Inner Work

The Application of Fourth Way Teachings

by

Rebecca Nottingham

Cover Art by Rebecca Nottingham

Second Edition

Originally published as "The Work: Esotericism and Christian psychology"

ISBN: 9798353653172
Printed in the United States of America.

Table of Contents

PART TWO – DYING

PART THREE – RE-BIRTH

Inner Work

Author's Note

I have studied and practiced the Fourth Way 'Work' for thirty-five years. I have done a small bit of teaching here and there and I have written two small booklets. One was called "The Fourth Way and Esoteric Christianity" which I wrote twenty years ago for Fourth Way students who had developed dangerous psychological conditions as a result of coming out of corrupt Fourth Way schools and organizations. The other was a six-week course for a church class in 2005 which became a class with just a few students for the study of Work ideas and their relationship to Christian teaching. I also helped to translate three books from their original French into English; "The Path of Initiation" by Karlfried Graf Durckheim, "The Prayer of Jesus," and "The Beyond Within" both by Alphonse and Rachel Goettmann.

I feel that it's important to note here that my understanding of this teaching has evolved since I last wrote on this subject. I do so now because it seems very important to me that the real meaning and aim of the Fourth Way Work not be lost among all of the misleading presentations of these ideas now so popular and widespread in the public marketplace. I also feel strongly that an ordered, progressive, step by step approach to the Work process is needed to preserve its original intent and keep students from getting lost in the confusion of misinterpretations and fraudulent 'schools' and teachers.

I was introduced to the Fourth way ideas by a friend who had been in a fraudulent school which was actually a cult. I read some of the original Fourth Way books like Ouspensky's "Psychology of Man's Possible Evolution," and

"In search of the Miraculous," among others, and found the ideas more than intriguing. I was immediately attracted to them but there seemed to me to be one serious flaw. Where was God in this new model of the universe and the ideas it taught? Then I was fortunate enough to find an old publication of Maurice Nicoll's "Commentaries on the Teaching of Gurdjieff and Ouspensky," and in them I found the missing piece that made the Fourth Way relevant and meaningful. Nicoll makes the connection between the Fourth Way Teaching and the inner meaning of Christ's teaching which explains the whole purpose of this path and where it leads. The "Commentaries" five volumes have incalculable value, and anyone interested in this path should investigate them. They are available online for reading and may still be available in published form. I also recommend Maurice Nicoll's other books – "The Mark," "The New Man," and "Living Time" for any serious student of this path.

Nicoll was a successful and noted psychologist during the first half of the twentieth century and he was probably one of the top theologians of the last century as well, but you won't find him among their ranks. He made no name for himself as a theologian while he quietly put together the most meaningful explanation of Christian ideas for his students. He is sometimes referred to as an esoteric teacher which is accurate, but the term is too vague to convey his contribution to the psychological understanding of the Gospels. His perspective reveals to us a dimension of Christianity that is hard to find in the literal parables and other scripture. It is powerfully enlightening and deeply meaningful.

I am not affiliated with any Fourth Way or Gurdjieff groups, schools, organizations, or individuals. Maurice

Nicoll was my only "teacher" through his writings. I've never belonged to a group or organization that taught the Fourth Way and I had no other teacher. I consider this to be an advantage because the aim of the teaching is lost in other Fourth Way books and organizations. Not that they have no value on some level, but Gurdjieff made a point of saying, "Don't confuse the vessel with the cargo." Maurice Nicoll gives us the cargo in the psychological "Work" of the Fourth Way without the distortions of the various vessels. And in that regard, I must say that I've never known of a legitimate Fourth Way group. There may be one, but for the most part you'd be taking a chance joining any group and should never lose sight of the aim of what Gurdjieff called *Esoteric Christianity*. That aim is increasing consciousness for the purpose of developing spiritual will.

INTRODUCTION

This teaching is called "The Work" and it is about the inner psychological meaning of Christ's teaching. It is a system of ideas and psychological practices derived from the Fourth Way system that originated with George Ivanovich Gurdjieff, interpreted by Peter Ouspensky, and taught by Maurice Nicoll. Gurdjieff was an esoteric teacher living and teaching in Russia at the beginning of the twentieth century. He and a small group of students walked out of Russia to avoid the war and eventually wound up in France where Gurdjieff founded another school which he called the Institute for the Harmonious Development of Man. Ouspensky was a Russian intellectual and philosopher and Gurdjieff's primary student. He wrote "In Search of the Miraculous" which is an organized presentation of what Gurdjieff was teaching. Maurice Nicoll was a highly regarded Scottish psychologist who was a student of both Gurdjieff and Ouspensky and studied with each of them individually. After years as a student, in 1931 he was asked by Ouspensky to teach the Fourth Way in London where he lived. This he did until his death in 1953.

Since this condensed version of the Work was taken completely from the "Psychological Commentaries on the Teachings of Gurdjieff and Ouspensky," and other books by Maurice Nicoll, I feel he deserves some special attention. He was born in Scotland in 1884. His father was a noted Scottish theologian and author, so Nicoll grew up in a religious Victorian household. He graduated from Caius College in Cambridge where he took a first in science and subsequently received his medical qualification at Saint Bartholomew's

Hospital. He also studied in Vienna, Berlin and Paris and then returned to London to private practice. He served as a Captain in World War I and was in charge of a hospital in Gallipoli. After returning from the war he took up his private practice again and joined the staff at the Empire Hospital where he authored numerous papers on medical psychology. In England he was considered a pioneer in psychological medicine. He was the protégé of Carl Jung until he met Ouspensky in 1921. His strong Christian background and training as a psychologist gave him a unique perspective and an ability to communicate the Work in terms that are understandable to the modern western mind with its appropriate intended aim. And his perceivable practice of it and its relation to the core of Christian teaching is revealed to us in every idea.

The Fourth Way system consists of three parts – the cosmology, the sacred dance movements, and the psychological Work. The cosmology is an enlightening, profoundly meaningful new model of the Universe. Its ideas and diagrams hold powerful concepts of universal scale, relativity, time, and Mankind's place in it, all in harmonious integration. It supports a sound Christology and reveals a God of pure and unchanging goodness. Maurice Nicoll thought that the Work shouldn't be taught without the accompanying cosmology. And while I agree in principle, I have chosen to only slightly skim the surface of it in this book because I want to focus on what is verifiable and pertinent to personal change.

The study of the cosmology is an intellectual undertaking and can only bring about a certain amount of mind-altering knowledge which doesn't have the power to create individual transformation without the psychological Work. However, it gives an invaluable idea of the magnitude of these ideas which may be necessary for some people. But not all of the cosmology is verifiable and one of the primary directives of this teaching is to *verify everything for yourself.* You are not asked to take anything on faith or blindly believe any idea. You must know and understand the ideas through your personal thoughts and reflections on them and you must know what you are doing and why and verify it with your personal experience of applying the ideas and practices to yourself. Nevertheless, I advise anyone who finds value in the Work to also study the cosmology at some time.

I don't address the sacred dance movements although they are impressive to see performed. Great emphasis is put on learning these movements in the official Gurdjieff Societies and affiliated Foundations around the world. However, one of the many reasons why I don't give them any significant consideration in this book can be expressed in a quote by Maurice Nicoll when he said that *"no amount of work on the body can produce psychological change."* This is something I have verified for myself, and it takes only a little thought to realize that to include the movements as part of a 'package deal' means excluding many people from the opportunity to find real, meaningful self-change. This means that putting the primary emphasis on the movements does a great disservice to the Fourth Way System not to mention the potential students seeking authentic change in themselves. Whereas the psychological Work excludes no one. Those who are unfit for it soon find they are uninterested or unable to pursue it. And there are those few perfectly nice people who are not meant for it.

It is the psychological Work that is the focus of this book because that is the transformative aspect of the whole teaching and therefore the most valuable. It can be used by anyone with a sincere desire for self-change but must not be mistaken for a magic formula for achieving power or mystical properties. As a matter of fact, undertaking this path for some personal worldly gain such as improving your golf game, or losing weight, or attracting someone's attention, will be a waste of time and perhaps even dangerous. You can't be sincerely involved in a teaching about self-transcendence for self-interested reasons. Your aim would be compromised and impure, and aim is very important in the Work. It's something you'll have to remember often.

The esoteric teaching about the psychological level of meaning in Christianity contained in The Work is the unchanging truth within its spiritual ideas. It is also the only possible evolution available to mankind. So, no matter how well versed you are in the Fourth Way cosmological ideas or how competent you may be in performing the movements, you will have no internal development unless you are practicing the psychological Work.

I'd like to say here that you can also have no understanding of these three foundational men or of the value of what they accomplished without practicing the Work. In applying the ideas to yourself you will begin to see the brilliance and the startling beauty of them and you will then be able to realize the quality of Being through which they had to manifest. That will forever change your conception of the teachers who brought it to us today and give relativity to the enormous amount of biographical and anecdotal material available about them. I caution you that most of it is something more like gossip or outright slander, and most is written by people who didn't know these men and have never practiced the Work or understood the teaching.

My aim in writing this book is to condense, organize and explain the brilliant writings of Maurice Nicoll in the "Psychological Commentaries on the Teachings of Gurdjieff and Ouspensky"; in particular, *The Work*. The Work is a perennial esoteric teaching about the possible evolution of an individual from a being driven by external life into a conscious individual guided by the developed spiritual will. While the five-volume Commentaries are vastly more informative they are not organized in any structured approach to the ideas of this teaching and the language from the beginning of the last century makes it slightly awkward to the current western mind. However, Nicoll has put into these papers to his students the real aim and practices of the Work of the Fourth Way, making the ideas practical and true to their intended purpose.

Gurdjieff, Ouspensky and Nicoll all called The Work "Esoteric Christianity" referring to the inner meaning of Christ's teaching. It's not a hidden or secret path but one of the inner truth Christ spoke of leading to personal development and realization of the essential self.

"The Work is the inner meaning of Christ's sayings and parables, and Christ's sayings and parables are what the Work teaches." Maurice Nicoll

So, even though the Work can be used by anyone regardless of religious affiliation for the purpose of inner development, I see no reason to change the original context given to us in Christian terms. Christ gave us this esoteric teaching for our era. Gurdjieff brought it to the western world within a much larger wholistic system including a new model of the universe combining science and religion. Ouspensky was essentially the interpreter of Gurdjieff's teaching, but it was Nicoll who put the psychological Work in its proper context and made it into a verifiable and comprehensible path for us today.

It is called the *Work* because it is you yourself who must study and apply the practices to yourself, and it is no easy task. It is work, real inner work, but it is worth it. If you feel like an artificial person; if you don't see how life can be explained in terms of itself alone; if you feel there must be another meaning to your life but you can't quite grasp it; if you long for something more authentic that you can't name, then this may be your path. Especially if you are a person who loves Christ with all your heart and soul but can't quite figure out how to follow him, to obey Him, to be holy as He was holy, then what you find here will delight you.

One of the most beautiful aspects of the Fourth Way is its concept of God. What is usually called God is called the *Absolute* in this teaching, and it is a unity, a singularity of *all goodness and all perfection*. The Absolute is not created, it precedes creation and is under only the law of its own will. Creation is a manifestation of the will of the Absolute which exists before, outside of and throughout all created things. The Absolute's good will toward even the least significant in creation is, for us, in the form of Jesus Christ who is a reflection of the perfect goodness of the Absolute. This understanding dispels any debate about original language and meaning regarding the term *Absolute*. There can be no dispassionate, cold or uninvolved God who gives us Jesus Christ.

"....the conception of God must not be sensual, based on an object. "God" is not to be thought of as an object apparent to the senses. We really have to understand here that "God", or put in Work terms, the Absolute, is not a created thing, for what is created needs a creator. "God" or the Absolute is uncreated; that is, not in Space and Time where visible creation exists. In this connection Christ expressly said, "God is a spirit: and they that worship him must worship him in spirit and in truth" (John 4:24). He is not an object of the senses living somewhere in Space, moment by moment. The

16

soul which is the function of relationship to your inner world and whose destination is to be turned away from the senses towards another order of truth called "God" must not be turned outwards to things seen, but inwards to realities that are invisible and cannot be touched, but can be fully experienced as inflows of new meaning." Maurice Nicoll

It is important to note here for the sake of relativity, that when Ouspensky was asked whether Christ taught the Fourth Way to which the Work belongs, his answer was that *"the way of Christ was something much bigger."* Don't be confused about the scale of the event that the life of Christ was in the history of the human race, and the teaching He taught. The Work is about His teaching. His presence among us is about God's perfect love, the Absolute's perfect goodness.

The Fourth Way teaching doesn't talk directly about God for several reasons. We speak of "God" very casually in our present age and we attribute all manner of earthly events to Him from the outcome of sporting matches to personal and natural disasters. We've lost the concepts of scale and relativity and reverence, and we fail to realize that the magnitude of God is far beyond the human mind's ability to comprehend. However, the whole aim of the Fourth Way Work is to prepare the inner self to be able to be directed and inspired by the Holy Spirit which is above us and is an extension of God's goodness to each of us individually. Through this experience we can know Him in a way that defies words. All language and previous opinions become irrelevant.

So, the Work is the only path in this system for psychological/spiritual evolution and it can be employed by anyone of any religious background, or even those with none at all, as long as they are sure that there is something higher in life than their self-gratification. That is the one requirement the Work has. You must believe in something higher than yourself. Otherwise, you have no way to move up above the self you are now to a new form of yourself, already within you, awaiting realization. Those who identify themselves as Christians will find deeper meaning and understanding and a strengthening of their faith including a verifiably real way to obey Christ's teaching, because you love him. Nothing could be more valuable.

In the Work each person must apply the practices to themselves conscientiously after learning what to do and why and how to do it. The aim of it is to increase your consciousness and reach a subsequent new level of understanding for the purpose of spiritual Rebirth. If applied rightly it will lead to authentic self-realization and an inner purity which are both necessary conditions for the possibility of higher consciousness and any further degrees of development. It requires long term conscious efforts that are of a psychological nature and at times are intensely difficult and painful to the ego and at the same time beautifully liberating. That is why it is called the Work. You must work for your inner development, and for a very long time.

One of the basic elements in this teaching has to do with the order in which the process of re-birth takes place. There is an order to this transformation and it's important to understand what it is and how it works. These steps begin with Awakening, then Dying, then Rebirth. And the process must follow this pattern because you must first of all awaken to what you are really like before you can know what parts of your psychological makeup must die in order to reach rebirth.

Awakening begins with new knowledge and the intentional employment of that knowledge. Then there must be death to what we have awakened to within us if it obstructs the path to the spiritual rebirth that is our rightful destiny. Without awakening there can't be any dying to the aspects of the self in the right way and therefore rebirth is impossible. This is one aspect of the teaching I have tried to address in structuring this book by putting the ideas of awakening first, the process of dying to the false self in the right way, second, with the aim of re-birth into a developed spiritual being, last.

"Awakening is not quite pleasant. One suffers and also is so very glad. You feel you are at last doing what you wanted, but had forgotten." Maurice Nicoll

The ritual of baptism is not enough to create actual rebirth because it is external and only symbolic of being submerged in the Holy Spirit. Instructions for actual inner transformation and spiritual development are found in the Gospels, in Christ's own words but they aren't given in an ordered form but are found in pieces in different places in scripture because it was written many years after His death by those who may have understood the teaching but did not convey that process in recording the history of His life. The Work puts these pieces in an order that can be understood and followed leading to being "born of the Spirit."

This teaching begins with self-study from a particular angle and in definite directions which must be learned. "Know Thyself" becomes the first line of action because if you don't know yourself how can you change yourself? And make no mistake, this Work is for the purpose of changing yourself, not changing the world. In all true esoteric teachings throughout history self-knowledge is considered the highest form of knowledge because it is the starting point of any possible change. Also, understand clearly that self-change means that you must necessarily become a different kind of person. You can't change and stay the same. The Work isn't something you can add on to yourself as you are, like

19

acquiring a new wardrobe or learning a new language. It is meant to change you into the authentic person you were born to become led by your developed Spirit. So be sure that changing the kind of person you are is a pervasive part of your aim and be prepared to work at it sincerely and diligently. If you do you will discover that this is the most beautiful path to enlightenment that exists.

"Now I wish to speak to you about how you work on yourselves and in what spirit you take the work. You cannot easily work from the ordinary religious ideas and moods. You recall the saying about new wine in old bottles. This work, this system of teaching, these ideas we are studying, are the most beautiful things you can possibly imagine —and they are new to us. No, they are far more lovely and beautiful than anything you can imagine. They accuse you only of being asleep. They hold no conviction of sin in them. They ask you quite gently to observe yourself. It is you yourself who must accuse yourself." Maurice Nicoll

PART ONE

✳✳✳

AWAKENING

"Awake thou that sleepest, and arise from the dead, and Christ shall give thee light." (Ephesians 5:14)

Inner Work

ESOTERICISM

"Now all true esoteric teaching exists because man is asleep and can awaken. That is why the Gospels exist. That is why this Work, which is a reformulation and sometimes called Esoteric Christianity, exists. But a man cannot be persuaded or dazzled by miracles or compelled by force to awaken. He himself can only awaken himself." Maurice Nicoll

Esoteric teaching has always existed in every age and epoch of known human history, some bits of which reach us in the form of myths or legends and even fairy tales. It is not a new idea or something imaginary, unreal or invented by a person as a result of their own thinking. It is not the latest psychological theory or instruction on steps you can take for the purpose of personal achievement. It is the most real thing in life. It comes to us from above the influences of life and has always existed in different forms suitable to the times, culture and people to whom it is given. But its teaching has always been the same teaching about mankind's condition and potential development.

Esotericism views Man as an unfinished creation that can become complete through certain kinds of internal efforts. Its unchanging aim concerns an individual's possible further evolution. It has to do with how to achieve the transformation or inner change known in some systems as rebirth or regeneration, but which in this system is called the attainment of Real 'I'.

All esoteric teaching is about the fact that we are born as self-developing organisms on the earth so that, by a specific kind of work on ourselves, we can reach something inherent in us called Real 'I'. In the form of Christianity, the object is to have what we call 'Christ' born within us. We are taught by Him that the "Kingdom of Heaven is within you." The Kingdom of Heaven in this system of esoteric teaching is called Higher Centers which are fully developed within us and are always speaking to us but we cannot hear them due to the coarse nature of our psychology which is turned outwards towards life and its influences. But it is possible to develop and organize the structure of our psychology so that we can put ourselves under different influences and hear from Higher Centers. Esoteric teaching shows us how.

All esoteric psychology has the central idea that this transformation is possible for Man; that he is capable of an individual further evolution through his own efforts and understanding. In this regard there have been many stages of Man and his contact with influences from a higher level, and from the esoteric point of view Man has degenerated psychologically and is now out of touch with Higher Centers in him and their influences on him. According to ancient teaching mankind originally lived in a golden age in a totally different inner state in which he could hear directly from Higher Centers, or from what is above him. But then he fell into a state of the "Sleep of Mankind" and due to the hypnotism of external life he can no longer hear or be taught directly from Higher Centers which are within him. He must now be taught from the outside, through knowledge given to his mind first of all. Do not mistake passing time with progress or evolution. Time means change but does not mean progress. So, from the esoteric point of view mankind has progressively degenerated not progressively evolved.

Man has two distinct sides – the side of knowledge and the side of his Being. When mankind had a more original internal condition he could be taught in a direct way that he cannot be taught today. Now he must receive new knowledge first through his intellect and then apply it to his Being. It is only in this way that he can develop his Being to enable contact with Higher Centers. In order to evolve a man must change his level of Being but to do so he must increase his knowledge so as to change his thinking. He cannot change if he retains his old way of thinking, his old attitudes, his old psychology. All this belongs to the side of man's knowledge but the problem is how to raise him on the side of his Being – on the side of good, because goodness belongs to Being, knowledge belongs to the mind. Without esoteric teaching to raise us up to some level of civilization mankind is basically barbaric. And one thing we must understand is that the civilization that we know today is based on the influences coming into the world through Christianity.

This teaching is based on overcoming the violence that exists at the lowest level in every person. The definition of 'violence' is vastly expanded in esotericism but the teaching about how to overcome it is perennial and has always been available to those who are sincerely seeking a purer and more authentic life.

In ancient scripture there are countless references to these ideas and representations of them in the form of parables and allegories and somewhat incomprehensible meanings within certain texts. For example, the Old Testament contains a record of different esoteric schools or churches that existed for a time and then perished. When an esoteric school or church carrying higher influences dies, it is followed by a 'flood' of violence and evil for a time until another school is established. In that regard we have the story of the school called "Noah" that survived the flood of evil carrying within it all the *good* necessary for a new beginning on the earth. So, whether or not there was a literal flood and a literal ark built to particular specifications is relatively insignificant compared to the psychological meaning of the story.

There are many levels of understanding in esoteric writings from the literal to the deepest spiritual truths. Reading sacred scripture with an understanding of esotericism will reveal layer after layer of meaning that can give you a new understanding and make perfect sense out of obscure texts. For example, the Parables within the Gospels have both a literal meaning and deeper psychological meaning as well, and one does not necessarily contradict the other although the literal meaning has often been so distorted by the many translations over the last two thousand years, that it sometimes appears to do so. They are simply on different levels of understanding. However, the psychological meaning, which is the spiritual teaching, is always about mankind's potential development or evolution. One important point to remember here is that *"esoteric"* does not mean hidden or secret although it has come to carry this implication in our modern culture. Esoteric means *"inner"* – the inner meaning of something. Therefore, we have been given the Gospels to tell us in which direction evolution should take place at this time in human history but they are given to us by Christ in parables - a literal way which also contains an inner psychological or spiritual meaning. In this system *psychological* and *spiritual* mean essentially the same thing and are interchangeable.

We have been given this teaching now because mankind has to be taught from outside himself, from the side of knowledge first, step by step, successive stage by stage, until the full light of understanding is reached. The mind is illuminated when it comprehends something it did not understand before. Understanding is the most powerful thing you can create because it opens you up to the influences coming from *Higher Centers,* meaning from what is above you spiritually speaking. So, you never need to feel lost or hopeless or overwhelmed by life if you hold on to the transformative ideas of esoteric teaching and apply them to yourself.

In the Lord's Prayer it is said, "Thy will be done on earth as it is in Heaven." One thing that this means is that the will of God is not done on earth otherwise we wouldn't have to pray for it to be so. However, esotericism is meant to connect man with God's will and to release him from his self-will. People are always trying to find evidence of God's will in the world looking through the perspective of the senses. They claim to see it in natural events like earthquakes and tornadoes and floods; they even claim to see it in wars and accidents when innocent people suffer and die, and in the world of politics and even of sporting events. But the will of God is not done on earth. *The will of Man is done on earth.*

To draw conclusions about God from what happens in life on earth is to have an entirely wrong perspective. Christ taught us that all people, good or bad, moral or immoral, suffer the same fate in life unless they 'repent'….. "Except ye repent, ye shall all likewise perish." But this word, 'repent,' which is mistranslated, does not mean to feel sorry or remorse. The original Greek word, 'metanoia,' means to think in a new way, but the Latin word 'repentare,' from which the English word 'repentance' is derived, means to 'feel sorry.'However, the Greek word metanoia contains no idea of pain or sorrow, it is above those emotional states and its essential meaning is *transformation of the mind.*

The Greek particle 'meta,' from meta-noia, indicates transference or transformation. It is found in common language like the words metaphor, which means the

27

transference of meaning beyond the literal words; or metaphysics, which is the study of what is beyond observable science; or metamorphosis, which refers to the transformation of a structure into an entirely new structure, as in a caterpillar into a butterfly or an egg into a chicken. So *meta* refers to a transformation - of meaning or of form, to something *beyond* the original meaning or form. The other part of the word is *noia*, from the Greek word *nous* which means *mind*. So, the word - *metanoia* - mistranslated as repentance - actually refers to a transformation of the mind which means an entirely new way of thinking. So, that scripture should read, "Except ye *think in a new way,* ye shall all likewise perish."

"And be not conformed to this world: but be ye transformed by the renewing of your mind, that ye may prove what is that good, and acceptable, and perfect, will of God." *(Romans 12:2)*

The point is that everything belonging to life and the external world that we receive through our senses, is not the place from which we can begin the transformation that Christ taught us as metanoia. Metanoia, or thinking in a new way, is the first stage of this transformation and the first idea to understand is that God's will is not done on earth.

"The system we are studying is the presentation in a form adapted to the times of something that was long ago understood, and long ago taught, about man and his inner possibilities. It has been understood and it has been taught not only since the beginning of known history, which is only a brief portion of all human history, but long before it, reaching us only in legendary form, in myths and allegories. The same teaching has always been given, but it has been given in different outer forms, in different dress, according to circumstances, according to the times and according to the

nature of the people or race to which it is being given. It has changed only in regard to the general state of people—that is, their level of being and the depth of their sleep in the things of the external senses and so of their opportunities in respect of inner evolution." Maurice Nicoll

WORK IDEAS

At the very beginning of the Work there is one overriding directive and it is: *Verify everything for yourself.* Don't take any of the ideas on faith, although you will sometimes have to suspend your usual thoughts, beliefs, attitudes and opinions until you can verify some part of the teaching for yourself. This you can only do through your own personal efforts to think about the ideas and employ the practices of the Work. But the firm instruction to verify everything can be considered a kind of safety net. You don't have to subscribe to anything you don't understand. However, as your understanding grows you will begin to see the Truth and Beauty and Goodness behind the Work and taste it for yourself.

There are three basic requirements in the pursuit of the Work: acquiring the knowledge of the ideas, applying that knowledge to yourself as a practical discipline, and a belief in something greater than yourself on a universal scale. The Work is not based on faith or even love, it is based on understanding. But if you have no belief that there is something greater than you are, some meaning to life other than your self-gratification, then you won't be able to do this Work. Because if you don't think that there is something above you in universal scale, you won't be able to move up to something higher than what you are now. The kind of understanding that the Work teaches is on a higher level than your ordinary understanding and you have to reach it for yourself through the effort of personal practice. Knowledge of the ideas alone isn't enough to cause any change in the kind of person you are. You must apply the ideas to yourself and practice them in order to gain any higher understanding – the kind that can't be taken away from you. However, if you do this, your newly found understanding will give strength to your faith if you happen to already possess it.

Many people have textbook knowledge of the Work ideas and can talk about them endlessly or even teach them to others without any practical experience of them or the accompanying understanding. Actually, those kinds of people only have information, not higher knowledge, but they may be able to regurgitate it convincingly to make it seem like they are knowledgeable. In the sincere pursuit of the Fourth Way these people are dangerous and they are legion. A person can study the Work for their whole life without ever applying the ideas to themselves. Yet it is only the practical application of the ideas to oneself that can result in higher understanding and the ability to teach. Information is fairly easy to come by in today's technical age but you can understand with your ordinary mind that a person can know the name and function of every part of a simple radio, but with the pieces laid out in front of them they can't build one. Building it requires more than information about the components. The same is true of the Work. First you must receive the knowledge contained in the ideas of the Work and you must think about them for yourself. Then you must apply that knowledge to your own psychology in order to gain new understanding. This is the first essential effort because the first general aim is to "Know Thyself." It is a simple but necessary beginning because you can't change yourself if you don't know yourself. In all esoteric teaching self-knowledge is considered to be the highest form of knowledge because it is the starting point of self-change.

Now, because the Work is about changing yourself you must have the desire for change as a prerequisite, so if you are satisfied with yourself as you are then the Work isn't for you. There are some perfectly nice people in the world for whom the Work isn't suitable so there's no condemnation implied. However, if you are seeking self-change you must be ready to accept that you can't change and stay the same. Change means becoming a different person and you can't become different if you are clinging to what you are now any more than you can move from one room to another in your house while holding on to all the furniture in the room you're in.

Then you must take the well-worn directive "Know Thyself" in a new way. Everyone presumes that they know themselves already; that they know what they say and do and think and feel and that they do all of these things intentionally and with full consciousness. All who think like this will be mightily insulted to be told that they do not, in fact, know themselves at all, but this is what the Work teaches. It tells us that we are not properly conscious of ourselves, first of all, and that all we say, think and feel happens in a state so subjective it is comparable to a state of sleep. So, the Work begins with increasing consciousness in an individual in order to develop understanding. This is the stage of awakening.

It's very important to understand the order of the stages that lead to rebirth. Christ taught and lived these three stages of *Awakening, Death and Rebirth* but they have been fragmented and disordered in the Gospels. Christ tells his people often to *"Wake up!"* and He gives us parables about how a seed must *"die"* in order to produce fruit, and how we

31

must be *"born again of spirit,"* to enter the Kingdom of Heaven. What we have to understand is that there is an order to this process of spiritual rebirth. An individual can undergo a definite and prearranged transformation in himself, a distinct development and real evolution or rebirth, if he knows and gradually understands what he has to do. Then he has to *die* to certain sides of himself and in a specific way. If he *dies* in the right way he may be born again as a *New Man or a New Woman,* provided there is anything suitably real and strong and worthwhile in him. But a person cannot see the right things to *die* to in himself unless he first *awakens*. So first we must *awaken*, which means to become conscious, and to do so we must be taught what we must work on in ourselves in order to awaken. This requires finding a teaching that isn't arbitrary or invented by ordinary people but one that comes from those who have awakened and left behind them instructions for those who also wish to awaken. Finding a teaching means seeking and you may have to spend a long time trying to find a real teaching in this world full of falsity. But if you do find one, don't make the mistake of thinking that your journey is over because it has really just begun.

So, this path begins with seeking, at least in your own heart because how can you find anything if you don't feel that something is missing or lacking in your life. If you don't believe that life is explainable in terms of itself and that there must be some other meaning to life that you can't quite articulate, then your heart is seeking. It is seeking meaning which is the right position to be in in relation to the Work. For if we seek nothing other than our own satisfied self-will, transformation will be impossible. And if we ask for nothing we will get nothing. This is the nature of the Universe which can be thought of as response to request.

To begin with the Work teaches that each person has two sides – an outer mind and an inner mind. The outer belongs to the external sense-based mind, the inner to the psychological mind. This is easily verifiable. The same thing viewed by the outer mind becomes quite different when viewed with the inner mind. If you are looking at a tree with your outer mind, this mind of the senses will reveal to you the trunk, the branches and the leaves. However, if you are looking at the same tree with the inner mind, for instance, the inner mind may be seeing the seasons passing, or associating it to an event related to the tree – a hanging or a first kiss, or you may glimpse its harmonious integration in the world of nature.

Ordinarily we look out at the world through our external mind which shows us what our external senses register according to their very limited powers. We see people and activity and eye catching, attention grabbing things and we suppose that this is the sum total of reality. But reality is not confined to our small range of the senses and does not only lie outside us. There is also the reality of our inner thoughts and feelings and desires and sufferings. This reality is even more real than the one given to us by our outer senses, or outer mind, and can only be comprehended by each individual himself. The inner reality lies invisibly within us and it is to this inner mind and inner reality that the Work applies.

It's important to note here that *inner is higher* and *outer is lower* and since the two minds, outer and inner, view the same thing in such completely different ways, they are discontinuous because they are on different levels. These levels are distinctly separate from one another like two rooms in a house on different floors or the rungs of a ladder. This discontinuity of the two minds shows us that their functions are different. The outer mind is turned towards the world, life and its affairs and events received through the senses. It is the sensual mind. It can be intelligent or stupid, well developed or weak. The inner mind is the psychological mind and its functions are more subtle and difficult to define. In most people it is like an unoccupied room whose door has never been opened. It isn't possible to move effortlessly from the outer to the inner mind yet some people assume they can easily do so, and when they are introduced to the Work and are told that a change of mind is necessary they use the ordinary outer mind as usual, and so get stuck. Without the understanding that the outer mind is 'lower' and the inner mind is 'higher' within them, they mix up these two orders of knowledge and get confused. Then the Work remains on the level of the senses.

The nature of the effort a person must make is to create a separation in their mind between the two orders of reality that meet in them. Man stands between two worlds – an external world that enters the senses and is shared by everyone, and an internal world that none of his senses know and is shared by no one. If a person has no sense of the discontinuous nature of the two minds they cannot move up to a higher level because they cannot let go of the sensual mind enough to step up to a higher rung in the *ladder of consciousness* existing within them. We all have levels of consciousness within us but just like the rungs of a ladder are discontinuous, so are the levels of mind, one higher than the other in the 'scale' of consciousness.

When the inner mind is opened up it can let in thoughts and insights that can affect the outer mind and eventually control it. This is how it should be. This is the right order. The inner mind, being much higher in quality and in *scale* should control the outer or lower. When the outer mind controls us,

34

it is in the wrong order and it makes us unhappy. But since what is higher can observe and comprehend what is lower, but the lower cannot comprehend what is higher, sensual thinking cannot open the inner mind. The object of the Work is to make you think in a new way but you cannot do this if you continue to use the outer mind in thinking about the Work ideas. You cannot casually get hold of the Work by adding some knowledge of it to your outer mind. It will never take root there. Only the right quality of *valuation* will make it grow in the inner mind. When you receive the Work inwardly it begins to open the inner mind because it is designed to do so. You then begin to see life with the inner mind and to think in a new way.

   "To think in a new way is the starting point of inner development. And this, as you all know, is exactly what the Gospels say. The Gospels are also "esoteric teaching" – that is, teaching about man's possible inner evolution. The Gospels say: "Unless a man thinks in a new way, he cannot gain the Kingdom of Heaven." This is unfortunately translated: "Unless a man repent." To think in a new way is to find new meanings and to be given new ideas is to have new thoughts." Maurice Nicoll

We do not see God with our outer senses. We do not see Him with our eyesight or hear Him with our ears or touch Him with our hands. However, the existence of God can be understood even though it is not seen. This is where *psychological thinking* comes in. It is another level distinct from sensual thinking. In what dimension is your memory, or how many dimensions has your thought? Is it three dimensional as your body is or the chair you are sitting on? Yet your thoughts are real to you. You may be deep in thought without being aware of either time or space. Where are you then? Your body remains visible in the dimension of

35

time and space that we all experience, but your thought is invisible to the senses and yet it exists and is real. Therefore, we must conclude that different dimensions exist and are open to us inwardly apart from the dimensions shown to us by our senses. In this inner private dimension, which each person has, thought and feeling are movement. For example, affection brings about nearness in this inner space and dislike will do the opposite. Affection is a state. Dislike is a state. As long as you feel affection for a person you are in a state that continues whether the person is physically present at one time or not at another. In this inner space that is private to each of us, there is no time as we understand it sensually. In place of ever changing and passing time there is *state*. Therefore, we get a glimpse of something in us outside of time – that is, state and inner space.

If we take ourselves as our bodies we get the wrong impression of ourselves. The physical body is the lowest level of ourselves through which all higher more internal degrees can exist. Your being is not your body. Your knowledge is not your body. Your understanding is not your body. The body does not think. The spirit of a person thinks and communicates through the body. If you take the lowest degree as the whole of yourself you will be missing something of the greatest importance. *You are not your body.* You are looking through it, seeing the world by means of it.

You have these two worlds that you experience – one is the external world given to you by your senses, the other is the internal world which is *how you take the external world.* The world of phenomena, that is, of appearances, is what the senses manifest to you, but the way you take the phenomenal world belongs to your internal world. Science, turned outwards by way of the senses, seeks to conquer and control nature. The Work, turned inwards, is about conquering

36

yourself, it is about *self-mastery*. That means it is about your internal side, full of thoughts and feelings and attitudes and opinions. The internal side of a person can only grow through what is true. It cannot grow through what is false. The external side, however, can easily grow through what is unreal and false. Therefore, some form of "truth" is necessary for change that will guide you and which must be applied to yourself with sincerity. The *truth* of this Work will prove itself to you if you sincerely apply it to yourself.

The ultimate formulation of the first Work-aim is found in the Gospels: *"Seek ye first the kingdom of God and His righteousness; and all these things will be added unto you."* *(Matthew 6:33)*. The reason for this is because all of the Work ideas and practices are aimed at purifying the inner person so that the Kingdom of Heaven, which is within you, above your current level, can be received. But the finer quality of energy belonging to the Kingdom of Heaven can't be received into the coarse, unclean environment of our ordinary consciousness. So, every practice is in essence seeking to create this purified state internally. For this you need new knowledge.

KNOWLEDGE

In regard to knowledge Nicoll tells us: *"Christ many times said to his disciples: "If you can bear it." And this means that great knowledge – knowledge about man and his situation on earth and his possibilities – is not something you can take in an everyday way, or join up with ordinary knowledge or think about as being foolish because it does not correspond to your opinion. Great knowledge demands great sacrifice and a long struggle with oneself."*

37

Gurdjieff said: *"A man must first of all understand certain things. He has thousands of false ideas and false conceptions, chiefly about himself, and he must get rid of some of them before beginning to acquire anything new. Otherwise the new will be built on a wrong foundation and the result will be worse than before."* Therefore, the Work begins with new Knowledge. Its ideas can make the difference between an ordinary person and possibly a conscious individual.

No one can gain knowledge without effort on their own part which is one aspect of sacrifice. The effort begins with giving external attention to the Work. At this stage the Work must enter through the senses and for that reason it can easily become mixed up with the ordinary knowledge that the senses show us. But it must move to a deeper level by distinguishing the different quality of the knowledge of the Work ideas and differentiating it from ordinary knowledge. Otherwise confusion can be the result. This kind of effort must be intentional. Intentionality makes it *conscious* effort. All life on earth must make effort of some kind in order to exist but this kind of effort is not conscious, it is mechanical. However, the acquisition or transmission of higher knowledge demands great effort both from the one who receives it and the one who gives it. It is extra effort, not required by life but required by the desire for transformation. It is this desire that will give you the will to pursue the Work.

There are only two sides of a person on which effort can be made and development is possible. The first is on the side of knowledge. That means thinking about the ideas of the Work, contemplating them, reasoning about them and forming your own individual sense of the Work, and this is the most important starting point. How you reason is a very important matter because how you think about the universe and your place in it can either shut or open the inner mind and heart.

The second side on which effort can be made is on the side of your *Being*. Being has to do with *goodness* and is something like the quality of your character. But effort on both these sides must be made simultaneously because together they create understanding. Understanding is the most powerful force you can create in yourself and it is the by-product of esoteric knowledge and the Work applied to your Being. So, these two sides - knowledge and Being - must be united in order to form understanding. Therefore, you must willingly apply to yourself the knowledge you receive because you can't work on your Being apart from the knowledge of this system. But you can't have any practical and realistic knowledge of this system unless you apply it to your Being.

Every bit of progress in the Work starts from your valuation of it because that is the basis of your desire for it. Desire activates the will and it is through the will that you begin to apply the knowledge to your being. *Then your understanding will grow through a union of the will of your being and the knowledge in your mind.* To have knowledge of these ideas is not enough to create transformation. You must gain understanding through the practical, experiential application of them to yourself. In the Work a person is defined by their understanding. In fact, the Work teaches that *you are your understanding.*

You can do the Work for superficial reasons or for deeper reasons; from different depths within yourself or from different motives. When a person does this Work for rewards or praise or position or obligation, or from a kind of conceit or pride, or for merit, for honors or from trying to please, or from imitation or fear – all these sources of the will are outside the real inner person so they aren't working *from themselves*. Their work then remains external to them and their understanding cannot grow. That makes sincerity and truthfulness with yourself another important cornerstone of this teaching. Goodness can only grow from these two.

MAN AS A SELF-DEVELOPING ORGANISM

One of the great teachings of the Work is that Man is part of an organic film covering the Earth made up of all life forms from microbes to whales and all plant life, as well. Man, however, has a unique position in this ecosystem. He is incomplete by creation but he can complete himself by specific kinds of efforts. This is not possible for any other part of organic life on earth which must remain as it is. However, Man is capable of inner change, of individual development or evolution into a different kind of man. All esoteric teaching as far back as known history is about Man being a self-developing organism and the idea that he can evolve.

First of all, Man is born with a physical body that is organized and which works in a miraculous way. But there is in him something that he can develop apart from his physical body. Man's psychological body, his inner side, first has to be developed by the influences of life and even then, it is not organized into a functioning unity. It takes conscious efforts to build up an organized psychology and only human beings are capable of making conscious efforts. Work efforts are conscious efforts and they are outside of the ordinary efforts everyone must make in life. Work effort isn't necessary for living life in the world. It is extra effort aimed at developing consciousness in order to create greater understanding and a unified higher level of Being that can hear and receive influences from 'above.' Those influences come from the Kingdom of Heaven within you and they are always trying to reach you but cannot be received at your ordinary level of consciousness, thus, the emphasis in the Work on developing consciousness. The result of this development or evolution is sometimes referred to as the attainment of Real 'I', which is what you were born to be. Real 'I' is your most authentic self, possessing qualities of individuality, conscience, unity and will that are unavailable in the undeveloped person.

In order to grasp this concept more fully we have to understand that Man has different levels of himself within him already existing. This is something you can verify for yourself quite easily by observation. Sometimes you are in a better state of yourself – benevolent, gentle, etc. - sometimes you are in a worse state – irritable, impatient, etc. *State is Level* in the Scale of Being, psychologically speaking. The evolution the Work speaks about is to a pre-existing higher state within you as a possible permanent level of consciousness. We all have had moments throughout our lifetimes when we touch these higher levels briefly. The Work can make this contact a frequent or even a permanent connection. It builds up a receptive apparatus that can *hear* internally and *understand* through developed *consciousness* and act with a unified *will*.

The universe is an ordered creation beginning with what the Work calls the Absolute. According to this teaching the *Absolute is All Goodness and All Perfection.* It is under no laws except the law of its own will. We usually call this concept God, but esoteric teaching finds this term too restricted and subjective. To most people God is outside them somewhere in the sky and acts and looks surprisingly like a human being. So, the Work refers to the supreme creative force of the universe as the Absolute. It pre-exists creation. Therefore, starting from the highest point in the Universal Scale we are taught that *energies* descend in an *ordered* manner to condense further and further until the result is matter. This descending order, from the finest energies to the coarsest matter in the universe, represents in material terms, 'scale' or levels. So, the universe also has *levels* in the scale of creation. For instance, there is the level of all galaxies taken together, and there is the level of our own galaxy, the Milky Way, and then the level of our sun as one of the six hundred billion suns in our galaxy, and the level of all planetary systems, the level of our Earth, the level of organic life on Earth, the level of Man as part of that organic life. All of these different levels of creation are under different laws, for example, all of the suns in the Milky Way are under a different set of laws than humanity is under – like laws regarding temperature and gravitational pull. The point is that the universe is ordered from the highest level to the lowest extending vertically, so to speak, and it represents scale. That is, one thing below another according to the laws that provide order, all in continual creation.

Man, as a child of the universe carries the stamp of the universe, so he also has different levels in scale within him. As a self-developing organism he can rise from one level to another in this vertical scale. Remember here that psychologically speaking, *level* means *state*. We already have lower and higher levels or states of ourselves within us and we can choose with our free will at what level we want to live our lives. Then we have to work for it. We have to give attention and thought to our place and meaning in creation. Life is short - a brief moment of opportunity full of confusion and distraction that goes by very quickly. We have to stop and think about what we are doing and how we are living. What is the source of our meaning? What is our ultimate purpose? And then we have to choose.

One of the biggest problems facing the human race is that individuals don't even know that they have this choice.

Everyone presumes that they are fixed as what and who they are, as they are, and that change refers to outer conditions and circumstances. You, who have found the Work now have a new option from which to choose. And if you choose this sacred path every detail of the Work will become alive to you because you will see it as instructions, a map, that can be followed if you wish to awaken to another life and another way of living on this earth.

Now it must be understood clearly that the Work is a psychological discipline, first of all. The efforts it requires are internal. All kinds of external disciplines in life do not develop people internally. For example, when a person joins the military they subject themselves to all kinds of regimentations and rules externally but this does not develop their internal side. Or, a person may bow down religiously a hundred times a day or have a perfect attendance record at church, but this will not change them internally. A person begins to change only when they begin to apply the Work to themselves and practice what it teaches them to do. No one else can do this for you. It is possible to teach someone this Work but it is not possible to make them work on themselves. You cannot gain consciousness or awaken through proximity or imitation or osmosis. You must work for it yourself. However, when you attain it, it is the most beautiful freedom from a prison you didn't even know you were in.

It is important to note that the Work must be done in a spirit of true affection for it in order to create real change because it is only through this kind of valuation that you can unite with truth. If you do it out of the conviction of sin, in a heavy, grave or sad way nothing can come of it. To work from the conviction of sin in a negative way can lead to a worse state of yourself than not to work at all. This is especially true if you show others what you are trying to do. You will remember what Christ said about fasting – that you should anoint your head and wash your face *"that thou be not seen of men to fast."* Doing the Work is a form of fasting.

"This Work, if you will listen to it and hear it in your hearts, is the most beautiful thing you could possibly hear. It speaks not of sin, but of being asleep, just as the Gospels do not really speak of sin, but only of missing the mark – the Greek word means that." Maurice Nicoll.

*   *   *

The Work teaches that we come down from a very high place in the universal scale into life on this earth so we are not only born from our parents. They create the vessel for the reception of this 'essence' that comes down from 'above' us in the universal scale. Life on earth is only a field for working on ourselves so that we can return to where we have come from. All this Work is to lead us back to our origins but we are down here on this planet because each one of us has something special in ourselves to work on, to struggle against with all our strength and all our faculties, and to overcome. So, it can only be seen as a great tragedy if we die without understanding why we are here and what the real reason is for our lives. The Work gives us the tools we need for this discovery. Then it is up to each of us to use them. This is what is meant by the term 'self-developing organism'. It is an opportunity given to everyone by birth and everyone is in exactly the right circumstances to be able to develop themselves. If you have been blessed to receive this Work into your life you will find that your circumstances provide the very things that you can use to work upon. But we usually lose ourselves very early in life. You have to take hold of yourself and think what is it that is important for you to work on, what you must do before it is too late.

External life exerts a strong hypnotic power over us and it is this we have to awaken from, otherwise your inner essential part cannot develop and you remain a slave to the events of external life. All the Work is aimed at putting your internal side into the right order with an organized and developed psychology and unified Real 'I' directing the external side. If you are governed by a developed internal side acting from psychological or spiritual understanding you will behave distinctly differently from a person governed by the changing circumstances of external life. You will have created within yourself a stable faculty that can withstand the ever-changing events of outer life and your habitual responses to them. As a result, you will understand your reason for being.

SLEEP

The Work teaches that every human being moves through their daily life in such a subjective state of mind that is nearly as intensely unreal as the state of literal sleep. The Gospels also teach this: *"The hour has come for you to wake up from your slumber, because our salvation is nearer now than when we first believed." (Romans 13:11) "Listen, I will tell you a mystery. We will not all sleep, but we will all be changed." (1Corinthians 15:51) "If he comes suddenly, do not let him find you sleeping." (Mark 13:36)* This condition is produced in us partly by the hypnotism of the senses which are glued to external life, and partly by the form of our individual psychology which, shaped by external influences, induces passions of various kinds in us, all having their basis in self-love.

"The self-love seeks to keep the man or woman asleep.
Awakening is thus rendered impossible for them. They are
"ever learning and never able to come to the knowledge of
the truth." Maurice Nicoll

We get excited about a special event, or angry at someone, or we feel resentful when we are insulted, we are frightened by our uncertainties, impatient when we are late, irritated when we are interrupted, and the list goes on. Life is a series of events one after another, overlapping each other, that we pass through. Each event solicits a response in you, particular to you. Other people may have a different response to the same event because they are under the influence of their own individually formed psychological sleep. However, each person is asleep in the Work sense. Each is asleep in their *habits of thinking*, i.e., thinking about the same things in the same ways; *habits of feeling*, i.e., recurring emotional states; *habits of talking*, i.e., gossiping, repeating the same stories, using the same phrases, the same words; *habits of attitudes and opinions*; habits of posture and gestures, of facial expressions, movements, body language and their *habitual ways of reacting to life and its events*. People are asleep in their imagination, in their illusions, their ignorance, their self-justifying, their constant inner talking and perhaps most of all, in their presumption that they are already fully conscious and aware of everything they say and do and think and feel.

Now this idea that we are all asleep and that you yourself are asleep is difficult to understand at first and it requires that you suspend your usual way of thinking while you contemplate the idea and try to observe it in others and in yourself, until you can verify it for yourself.

Taking an ordinary example, let's say that a man wakes up early to the sound of his alarm clock. He is immediately bothered to be startled awake from a deep sleep. Then he remembers that he is waking up early so that he can go fishing on his day off, and he is suddenly happy at the thought and excited by it. He jumps into the shower and then gets shampoo in his eye which stings and angers him. As he is dressing he discovers that his favorite fishing shirt is dirty and he is immediately irritated at his wife because she didn't wash it for him even though he asked her to, but as he goes into the kitchen to confront her he smells the morning coffee and sees that she has also awakened early to fix him breakfast and his anger melts away and is replaced by appreciation. That first sip of coffee sends a wave of pleasure through him until the next moment when the dog jumps up and the hot coffee he was just appreciating splashes on his second favorite fishing shirt. Angry again he curses the dog and is frustrated at the thought of finding another shirt. As he is finally dressed and fed he feels a sense of wellbeing and love for his wife who has made his breakfast and wishes him well on his fishing trip. Then he can't find his fishing tackle and loses his patience looking for it, but feels relief when he finds it until he opens the door to see that a downpour has begun and lightening is flashing. Angry again he slams the door, curses and begins to feel sorry for himself thinking that this always happens to him. When he makes plans something always spoils them and his day off is ruined.

I could go on with this example but the point is that this man is asleep in his own world of reactions to external events, his self-interest and self-love. Everyone functions in this manner. We react automatically like a stimulus-response organism; we don't act consciously. This is the condition the Work calls the *Sleep of Mankind.* However, this man believes, as does every individual, that he is fully conscious, that he acts from his own volition, and is perfectly aware of himself and what he is doing. One of the things that keeps him from seeing his true condition is imagination. He imagines that he is unified and that all of these different states of himself are one unified self; he imagines that he possesses self-awareness, and that he acts intentionally, knows who he is and what he is doing. Therefore, he cannot change.

We are all swept up in the current of life and its activities. Our attention is being snagged by one thing after another, our emotions changing in response to events. There is no unity in us and no room for God. Even when we are not talking out loud, our thoughts are chattering away, mostly concerned with what we like and what we dislike, whether we approve of or disapprove of 'whatever' - the neighbors, our friends, co-workers, family members, the boss, the weather, the mayor, our lunch, our appearance, etc. We are continuously talking in our minds, carrying on a running conversation with ourselves about what we think and how we feel. We are thinking about the past and imagining the future. We are worrying and complaining, criticizing, speculating and expressing our opinions about everything that passes through our daily lives. We are daydreaming and fantasizing and thinking about what we want and don't have, or what we have and don't want. We are dwelling on our dissatisfactions with life, our circumstances, our limitations, other people and ourselves. Also fears plague us – worry, dread, insecurity, imagination about dangers, anxiety and guilt. Thoughts and emotions evoke each other in response to the changing experiences in the external world and the result is a continuous noise in the mind. We are like a two-way radio with the talk button stuck on send. We are constantly emitting noise and because of that we are unable to receive. This is why we can't hear the Holy Spirit who is always reaching out to us, seeking us, offering inspiration, comfort, insight and guidance. If you want to hear from what is above you, you are going to have to stop making so much noise.

On top of it all we are unaware of our condition which is why it can be called a kind of sleep. The most instrumental factor keeping us locked in this condition is that we don't know that we have a choice or even that there is a choice. We have to learn to recognize that we each live in a fog of self-interest, self-emotions and self-will and we have to learn that we can choose to live in the freedom of God's will instead. Then we have to exercise self-control to work against imagination, lying to ourselves, justifying ourselves, pride, vanity, fear, self-complacency, spiritual laziness, and rebellion from our flesh. Being spiritually asleep means missing the mark. It means missing our reason for being alive – reunion with God.

Metanoia is the cure. (*Romans 12:2*) *"Do not conform any longer to the pattern of this world, but be transformed by the renewing of your mind."* This word 'metanoia' has been mistranslated as 'repentance'. However, feeling sorry about your condition of sleep is not the path to transforming it. Becoming conscious of your condition of sleep and working against it is the only way to free you from it and make transformation possible.

This is why one of the first things the Work teaches is that human beings are not properly conscious. Therefore, the primary aim of the Work is to increase consciousness. This expansion of consciousness can only take place at the expense of our usual feeling of ourselves and that leaves us with a peculiar feeling of not knowing who we are at times. This phenomenon is what I call 'psychological vertigo'. You will find at such times that you will talk less, for instance, or you may not recognize the person presenting themselves as you but is not representing your true self. Although this can be temporarily disconcerting, it also makes room for the authentic self to grow. If you continue to practice what the Work has taught you at these moments, the Work will hold you up until your internal or psychological side has adjusted and is more developed and stronger.

As we are, we attribute full consciousness to ourselves and to others, as well. We talk and behave, think and feel and judge on this assumption, which gives us no peace because it is a sense-based mistake. In reality we cling to our usual and familiar condition of sleep and we especially cling to the sources of our distress and even resent being separated from them. Why we so adamantly hold on to those things that make us suffer is a mystery but maybe this happens because we define ourselves by just those things and have an unconscious fear of the loss of identity we would experience if we were deprived of our anger and bitterness, our complaints and resentments and judgements. Without these, who are you? This feeling you have had of yourself - this small, restricted, over sensitive bundle of pride, vanity, illusions, prejudices, and wrong attitudes, will gradually disappear as you practice the Work which will reveal your more authentic self. The increase of consciousness of this new sense of yourself brings with it a great feeling of relief because no one can have any inner peace or escape from persistent inner agitations as long as their current feeling of themselves remains unchanged.

Part of the aim of awakening is to give the possibility of a new unified self with a unified spiritual will, acting from Real Conscience, Objective Consciousness, and stable Individuality. That possibility is why the study of the *Sleep of Humanity* is a central and preliminary idea. One you must verify for yourself through observation.

"The direction that can lead somewhere is awakening from sleep. In every small part of time, some people are ready to awaken. If they do not try to do so, they block the way for others. It is like a ladder on each rung of which people are standing. If those above do not move up, those below cannot move. Awakening is the individual task of everyone. But only a few can awaken at a time or find the possibilities offered them. If these begin to awaken the effect spreads and others begin to understand what work means and what awakening means." Maurice Nicoll

THE FOUR LEVELS OF CONSCIOUSNESS

To help us understand our position as part of sleeping humanity in the Scale of Consciousness the Work gives the following diagram showing the levels of consciousness possible for human beings:

States/Levels		
4th State	**Man Awake**	
Man #7	Light	Objective
Man #6	Help Available	Consciousness
Man #5		
3rd State	**Man Awakening**	Self-Remembering,
Man #4	Light	Self-Consciousness,
	Help Possible	Self-Awareness
2nd State		Waking State
Man #3	**Man Asleep**	(Psychological Sleep)
Man #2	No Help Possible	
Man #1	Darkness	
1st State		Literal Sleep

First state is physical, literal sleep. Second State is what the Work calls the *Waking State* in which we pass most of our lives, not properly conscious but believing that we are. In this state we walk and talk, work and read books, eat and socialize, fight and even war and kill one another. It is characterized by the illusion that we are fully awake and that we always act and talk consciously and always know exactly what we are doing. All of humanity belongs to these first two levels of consciousness. All are considered asleep in the prison of the sensual mind which is like a kind of death.

The Third State is a level above us that we can only obtain by specific kinds of efforts. It is characterized by a state called *Self-Remembering* and it has Self-Awareness. This is the state we occasionally experience as a gift and a sign that some higher degree of our self exists, but it is a state that is not a permanent condition. It has different degrees of permanence as we work on ourselves toward a higher form of consciousness that is fixed. However, in Third State we can fall back into Second State, easily at first. But with increasing consciousness we have a stronger stance in Third State and cannot fall back so easily.

The Fourth State is the state where man is wholly objective and sees things as they really are with no illusions, or pretense. In some disciplines this state is sometimes called 'Enlightenment' but it is the same level characterized by the same attributes in anyone who achieves it and those attributes are permanent. Those individuals who have developed consciousness to that extent – Man #5, #6, and #7 - all know the same truth; they all understand the world and the things of life in the same way. And they understand each other no matter their origins. In that regard it must be said here that different religions, cultures or races cease to exist in the commonality of Higher Consciousness.

"I heard it once said that one of the most difficult things for a man who reaches that stage of development where he begins to come in contact with the highest teaching is that he has to give up his "religion." He may feel himself a very good "Catholic", a very good "Quaker", a very good "protestant". A very good "Mahometan", and so on – i.e. he rests on this basis, thanking God that he is not like other people, other unbelievers. In the highest stages of inner evolution all such distinctions have to go completely. Perhaps you can think for yourselves how this must be so."
Maurice Nicoll

In other words, there can be no differences in the perspectives belonging to fully conscious people, no separate interpretations of conscience in unified higher conscience, no judging of one religious doctrine as superior to another among those who have transcended doctrine. The level of Being belonging to the Fourth State is above these separations. If you recall Christ said*: "Two men went up into the temple to pray; the one a Pharisee, and the other a publican. The Pharisee stood and prayed thus with himself, God, I thank thee, that I am not as the rest of men, extortioners, unjust, adulterers, or even as this publican. I fast twice in the week; I give tithes of all that I get. But the publican, standing afar off, would not lift up so much as his eyes unto heaven, but smote his breast, saying, God, be merciful to me a sinner. I say unto you, This man went down to his house justified rather than the other: for every one that exalteth himself shall be humbled; but he that humbleth himself shall be exalted." (Luke 18: 10-14).* A fully conscious person recognizes that we are all like the publican, none better than another from the point of view of absolute perfect goodness, and all in need of the mercy of God, and therefore

cannot hold their own religious tradition as better than
another.

The only *right way* to this Fourth State is through the
development of the Third State of consciousness or Self-
Remembering which belongs to the Third State.

Now the hard truth to grasp here is that help from above,
from the Fourth State, from what the Work calls Higher
Centers, which is the Kingdom of Heaven within you, can
only reach down into the Third State of consciousness. It's
not that this help isn't extended to each one of us at all times,
it's that we cannot hear it or receive it in our noisy subjective
Waking State, and because of the illusion that we already
possess this level of consciousness and can access it by desire
or determination alone. The truth is that we have to raise
ourselves by specific practices to the Third Level of
consciousness in order to receive the help which is available
to us. This Third State is the natural right of Man, and if Man
doesn't possess it, it is because of the wrong conditions of his
inner life. This Third Level of consciousness, or Third State,
is where practicing the Work leads.

Consciousness is hard to define and a person may not
understand what an increase in consciousness can possibly be
like. Even if they are willing to admit that they are not
properly conscious they cannot see what it means to increase
consciousness and can feel utterly helpless through sheer
ignorance. Consciousness can be thought of as a very high
quality of energy in the scale of energies. Although it may be
something like perspective, it is not thought, or feeling, or
sensation, or movement, it is not memory, and it is not a
psychic process. Through consciousness you become aware
of these things within you, but consciousness can exist
without content. It is unique, something like a group of high
frequency vibrations, and like light it exists whether or not

we perceive it. It is not this light that has to be increased but our contact with it. It is the *receptive point* of our personal consciousness that has to be changed, in effect lifted up into the light. Our individual consciousness can only be increased through *conscious efforts* by the use of the small amount of consciousness we are each given.

"*To awaken is to become more and more conscious by letting in consciousness into the dark places....within us. It is said in John that "the light shineth in the darkness and the darkness comprehendeth it not". So it is with everyone who is given the Work, which is Esoteric Christianity – that is, its inner meaning – and does not open the door to it. He does not let it in. He sees the light but, not turning it inwards upon his own darkness, remains without comprehending it.*"
Maurice Nicoll

This inner darkness which we all have refers to what we are unconsciousness of within ourselves. It does not refer to something evil lurking within your subconscious. The darkness of sleep is like a kind of death but not necessarily evil. The Work does not ask you to go searching around in yourself to come up with evil thoughts or evil feelings that you can attribute to yourself. It asks you to shine the light of consciousness objectively on your inner psychology to reveal its workings to yourself. Some of them may indeed be evil, but darkness means only what you are unaware of. Shining the light of consciousness into your psychology is an intentional conscious act and will therefore increase your consciousness and self-awareness. If we were already fully conscious, we would not need this Work. It would not even exist. But we are not fully conscious and in the Waking State all sorts of lies pass as truths. Yet we are all born with the capacity to live in the Third State of consciousness where lies are impossible and deception does not exist. To be more conscious, more awake, means that you have more light and so perceive more, and possess a degree of inner purity that does not lie and can discern truth.

"For most people, even for the educated and thinking people, the chief obstacle in the way of acquiring self-consciousness consists in the fact that they think that they possess it.... It is evident that a man will not be interested if you tell him that he can acquire by long and difficult work something that in his opinion he already has." Gurdjieff

SEVEN KINDS OF MAN

The Work also teaches that there seven different kinds of Man belonging to the four different Levels of Consciousness. Man #1, Man #2, and Man #3 all belong to the First and Second Levels. This is *sleeping humanity* either in literal sleep, called First State, or in Second State, called the Waking State. It is in the Second State that Man lives his life, works, walks, talks, governs, and teaches, creating all kinds of suffering and chaos, and believing that he is fully awake. The only difference in these three types of Man lies in the fact that they each have the *center of gravity of their being* primarily in one of the three corresponding "Bodies of Man" given to us by esoteric Christian teaching. Those are the Physical Body, the Emotional Body and the Intellectual Body. This idea we will go into further in a following chapter, but for now to illustrate what this idea means let's say these three kinds of Man are walking together and they come upon a horse.

Man #1, with his center of gravity in the physical aspect of life will have a corresponding perspective, for example: thinking how big the animal is, wondering if he could ride it, how fast it can run and whether it is dangerous. Man #2 has his center of gravity in his emotions and will be thinking something like how beautiful the animal is, how appealing the form of the body, how soft the eyes, and how bad the smell. Man #3 whose center of gravity is in the intellect will have the response of wondering what other animals belong to the same species, or speculating about what animal it evolved from, how do the muscles work together in unison to produce speed, to what extent it can be trained, what it eats and in what quantity each day.

All of these categories of people are asleep, each in their own perspective generated by their center of gravity's relationship to the horse. They live in the darkness of their individual sleep and they don't understand each other. Having their center of gravity in one or the other of the functions of the Bodies of Man renders them blind to other perspectives and therefore, one sided. Remember that all three kinds of Man at the First and Second level of consciousness are Asleep. They make up *all* of humanity and none has an advantage over another in the possibility of evolution which body your Center of gravity is in does not signify intelligence or level of Being.

There are a very small number of individuals in the vast body of humanity that are trying to awaken or have to some degree already awakened. These few are Man #4, or what the Work calls *Balanced Man*. He is at the Third Level of consciousness which is called Third State. Balanced Man is not one sided. He has worked on and developed all his functions so that they can do everything his different 'centers' – physical, emotional, intellectual, - make it possible for him to do, acting with the appropriate center, quality and quantity of energy. Man #4 possesses self-awareness, self-consciousness and he *"Remembers Himself."*

He sees the life he led as Man Asleep as something going on far below him at a lower level and it no longer affects him. People at this level of consciousness understand each other and since they have self-awareness they no longer judge each other. Most importantly, they can receive help and influences from above.

Man #4, in the Third State, is the bridge to Conscious Man numbers 5, 6, and 7, at the Fourth Level of Consciousness or Fourth State. This higher conscious Fourth State is what we are aiming for in the Work. When we are in Third State we can hear and receive influences from the Conscious Circle of Humanity above us, made up of Man #5, Man #6, and Man #7, and which we commonly call the Kingdom of Heaven.

This Conscious Circle of Humanity is always speaking to us but it is only in Third State that we can hear it. That is why the whole of the Work is a roadmap to the higher, awakening Third State where we can 'hear' higher influences and where light and help can reach us.

Not that our personal work efforts are finished, but we will be given help and guidance from above.

Adding these seven different kinds of Man to the diagram of Levels of Consciousness gives us the following new diagram:

FOUR LEVELS OF CONSCIOUSNESS
SEVEN KINDS OF MAN

States/Levels

4th State	**Man Awake**	
Man #7	Light	Objective
Man #6	Help Available	Consciousness
Man #5		
3rd State	**Man Awakening**	Self-Remembering,
Man #4	Light	Self-Consciousness,
	Help Possible	Self-Awareness
2nd State		Waking State
Man #3	**Man Asleep**	(Psychological Sleep)
Man #2	No Help Possible	
Man #1	Darkness	
1st State		Literal Sleep

Although it may appear that Man #3 is above Man #2 and #1 in consciousness this is not so. These three kinds of Man are categorized according to their *Center of Gravity* which refers to how they relate to life. Man #3 whose center of gravity is in the intellect may be a very stupid man but one whose perspective is his version of logic and reason. Man #2 whose center of gravity is in his emotions can be an artist to some degree if he is somewhat developed, or if he is not he will simply be constantly liking or disliking, loving or hating everything because this is the behavior of emotions. Man #1 whose center of gravity is in the physical body may be easily satisfied by eating, sleeping and sex, or he may have a high intellect or a noble character. The point is that none of these first three kinds of Man has an advantage over another in regard to consciousness. All three live their lives in First and Second States and so *all are equally asleep*, in darkness, with no internal help available because their condition of sleep makes them deaf to the influences coming down from above. Humanity is composed of these three kinds of Man and although everyone will have rare flashes of higher states at times during their life, they will fall immediately back into Second State and will remember nothing, or very little of those experiences.

All of the seven levels of consciousness exist within us and are accessible to each one of us to one extent or another. This shows that Man has *scale* within him. The universe has scale within it and as a child of the universe man has scale in him, also. That is why this Work is possible. Without scale there would be no higher state of yourself for you to evolve into. And that is why all Work efforts are directed at attaining the Third State of Consciousness, or becoming Man #4, which is our natural right. If all humanity were in this Third State all wars would stop immediately and people would understand one another, but this cannot happen. Some literature and even some new religions speculate on this proposition believing that some cosmic event will suddenly awaken all of mankind at once. As lovely as that sounds the fact is that there is no mass psychological evolution, there is only individual evolution. So, each one of you can only evolve yourself, you can only change yourself, you cannot change the world. The Work is not for people who want to change the world. It is for those who wish to change themselves.

The change we are talking about is becoming Man #4. If you live and die in a state of sleep, you will never realize the most important thing there is to strive for. As you can see from the diagram, Balanced Man #4 is at the level above us and he has self-consciousness. He remembers his authentic self and his source. There is 'Light' at this level and the influences coming from above can be discerned. What we are given at this level is individual and comes as a gift - not one you can generate but one you can put yourself in a position to receive.

However, all of this means that you yourself will have to invest hard conscious efforts over a long period of time to awaken. The attributes belonging to Conscious Man- those of, Real 'I', Real Will, Real Conscience, Objective Consciousness, and Individuality, are shared by Man #4 but in him they are not unified and fused into something permanent as they are in Conscious Man.

There are some common misunderstandings about Balanced Man due mostly to external, sense-based thinking. Nevertheless, you will frequently come across the same misinformation in the world of Fourth Way groups. The thinking behind these distortions is something like the idea that in order to evolve you must fully develop all your centers – meaning that you must be able to think like a genius, have only the most genteel emotions, and perform like an athlete. Under this misconception students are made to perform pointless mental exercises that lead to nothing, made to listen to and/or surround themselves with only the finest quality classical art and music, and expected to master complicated dance movements said to have esoteric meaning. They may or may not have meaning but it doesn't matter because no amount of physical effort or mental acuity or swimming in a sea of Bach will produce any internal, psychological growth. So, nothing could be more mistaken.

However, the idea of balancing your centers does mean developing them, especially your less developed ones, to the extent that is as highly functional as they can be. This will take conscious efforts to do things you would not ordinarily do. If you are an intellectually centered person you may have to learn how to do practical chores or if you are a physically centered person you may have to read a book, and if you are emotionally centered you may have to take up carpentry or clean something. With consciousness #4 Man can use all his centers and use the appropriate center for the appropriate task with the appropriate energy. This means functioning with more efficiency and it conserves energy. Conscious efforts take energy and we ordinarily waste a good deal of ours in the disorganized malfunctions of undeveloped, unbalanced centers. For instance, digging a ditch or doing the dishes or memorizing mathematical tables with interference from the emotions, like resentment, wastes energy. Balanced Man #4 understands how and why and when to use each center. This is the real meaning of balancing your centers. *It means an appropriate use of the developed functions of the centers that comes with the organization of your psychological/spiritual body.*

That being said, becoming #4 Balanced Man cannot be overestimated. Life does not produce him. It is only through work on himself that he can reach this state and it is an unassailable fact that there is no other *right way* to becoming Conscious Man. The path of the Work to this higher state builds the right foundation for further development and fusion, or crystallization, into a unified permanent state without distortions. Balanced Man is the bridge between Sleeping Mankind and Conscious Mankind and is therefore of the greatest importance. Conscious Man is built on Balanced Man. A man must be #4 Man before he can be Conscious Man. A person who reaches the level of Third State cannot remain what he was. Because his level of consciousness and his qualities have changed, his feeling of himself will change and his former life will not have the same psychological '*taste*'. His emotions will be purified and so he will have different feelings and not be tormented by any previous feelings that caused him distress in his life as a Man Asleep. This kind of change means change in everything. Remember, *you cannot change and remain the same.*

"The Balanced Man, sums up the teaching and explains its existence, and, standing above the mechanical living of this life, is open to respond to another life, the living of which is our right – a right neither inborn nor acquired, but pre-existent in our Essence by creation. For we were created to become conscious; and to attain to a degree of consciousness sufficient to reach even the farthest outskirts of the Conscious Circle of Humanity is something incommensurable with anything that life offers. It makes all the affairs and situations of life seem as nothing, or near to it." Maurice Nicoll

THE CROSS DIAGRAM

"And if we could remember ourselves and did remember ourselves and did touch the Third State of Consciousness we would know this quite well already; and, knowing it, know that our life lay above us, and not behind us or ahead of us – a knowledge that shifts the usual feeling of oneself which is horizontal and not vertical. By horizontal I mean what is based as a horizontal line of past, present and future, and so on our idea of time: and by vertical I mean based on scale,

and on above and below, on higher levels and lower levels, and on values which are not connected with time but with states." Maurice Nicoll

To further define the levels of consciousness the Work gives us the ideas of Time and Scale of Being expressed in the following Cross Diagram:

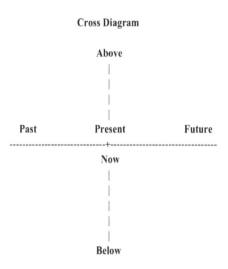

The horizontal line represents chronological time – past, present and future. The vertical line represents Scale of Being from lower to higher, in the total Universe of meaning. There is no concept of time in it. Being is the quality of what you are. The vertical line shows *position* in the infinite scale of *Levels of Being*. In the vertical line there is no past, present or future, instead there is *state* or *level* or *quality*. The point where the horizontal line of Time is intersected by the vertical line of Scale of Being is *now*. Every moment of a person's life can be represented this way. It is only a sense of the existence and meaning of the vertical line that gives the feeling of Eternity. Eternity and chronological Time meet in Man at every single moment at the point called *now*. This is what is meant by the teaching that "state means place". The quality of your state in every moment of *now* refers to your place in the Scale of Being at that moment.

Every state finds its own level in the vertical scale according to its 'density' or quality. Higher states have a finer quality of energy, they are less dense. Human beings, born as self-developing organisms, can evolve and rise from one point to a higher point in this scale. Scale means *Ladder*. You will recall that in the first few books of the Old Testament we find the example of Jacob's Ladder. The ladder represents the Universe as seen in its vertical height and depth, and Jacob represents Man Asleep at the bottom of the ladder and the level of development existing in him.

"And he dreamed, and behold a ladder set upon the earth, and the top of it reached to heaven; and behold the angels of God ascending and descending on it." (Genesis 28:12)

All evolution means to pass from one point to a higher point in this scale. To pass from one point in the vertical line to a higher point a thing must be transformed. It must become different from what it was at a lower level. A person, being capable of inner change, is not seen as a fixed point in this vertical scale and, therefore, Work aim has to do with the vertical line. It has nothing to do with Time, however *"We each have our allotted span of life in Time appropriate to changing our being." Maurice Nicoll*

This idea gives a whole new dimension of meaning to the phrase "wasting your time".

"The vertical line represents position in the scale of states of being, in the level of understanding and the quality of knowledge. It is so necessary to gain some preliminary conception of the significance of this vertical direction, that does not lie ahead of us, in the future of Time, in next year or the next century, that does not lie in either Space or in Time,

but lies in another dimension – namely, above us." *Maurice Nicoll*

The significance of this idea is that your Real 'I' is at a higher level of Being, a higher level of consciousness, a higher level already existing within you. *It does not lie ahead of you in chronological time, it lies above you in every moment.* Real 'I' can only be reached by the inward movement of lifting yourself up, by ascent out of sleep to a higher level of consciousness. Real 'I' is fully developed, awaiting you at a higher level called in the Gospels "The Kingdom of Heaven," and in the Work terminology, the Conscious Circle of Humanity. Attaining it is the aim of the practical side of the Work.

The vertical line represents the line of transformation from one level to another in the Scale of Being. It cuts at a right angle through the horizontal line representing chronological Time which is the line of change. The vertical line is timeless. Transformation is not the same as change in Time. Everything *changes* in Time but the passage of time does not *transform* a thing. In this system *transformation* is the real meaning of *evolution* and it does not lie along the horizontal line of Time but is a necessity on the vertical line. All of the teaching in the Gospels is about ascending the vertical line to reach the Kingdom of Heaven because an individual can rise in this vertical scale. *"A higher state of yourself does not lie ahead of you in Time, it is above you now, and in every moment of your life. This is what intelligence means in the Work – the position of a thing in the Scale of Being."* *Maurice Nicoll*

LEVEL OF BEING

The idea shown in the Cross Diagram requires that we understand more fully what 'Being' means. In general, a person's Being is made up of everything in their character. More subtlety it has to do with goodness and the *quality* of your character which is defined by the quantity of goodness in it. We all have a range of different Levels of Being in us. You can verify this by noticing that at times you feel kind hearted or gentle and at times you feel almost in a violent rage, but your general level will balance out somewhere in between. You can observe that some people have a very low level of being evidenced by many forms of violence and negativity or even criminality. And there are some who have a very high level of being close to saintliness. The quality of your being belongs to the vertical line. Where the vertical line cuts through the horizontal line marks the point of your level of being at that moment in Time. And most importantly, *what you experience in Time is the result of your Level of Being.*

Your life will be according to your level of Being. If your being changes then your life will change accordingly. The great teaching of the Work regarding this idea is that:

YOUR BEING ATTRACTS YOUR LIFE

If your level of Being changes then the horizontal line of Time will pass through the vertical line of Being at a higher level. Levels are discontinuous like the rungs of a ladder - they don't merge. That means that what exists on one level does not necessarily exist on another. You can think of it as something like telephone wires strung between poles, one above another. A flock of birds lands on the different wires.

Without getting more graphic you can imagine that a bird landing on the bottom wire will find a different experience than a bird that alights on the top wire.

Mankind lives by meaning. Meaninglessness is a death dealing condition. As we ascend in Being meaning is transformed. All people receive meaning according to their personal level of Being which determines their receptivity of meaning. Meaning comes from above, derived from Absolute meaning, descending from level to successive level, from higher to lower, and it is different at each level. Transformation of meaning is possible for a person as their level of Being changes. If this happens, where they had understood only one thing obscurely, they will then understand a thousand things distinctly. An analogy would be like different floors in a city skyscraper. If you are on the fifth floor you have a view that shows you a perspective of the street below and the surrounding buildings. But, if you are on the top floor the view revealed to you is much more expansive with many more things in it. Perhaps you can even see beyond the city or see the horizon. You can see how the surrounding streets intersect, how the other buildings are laid out, if there is a mountain range, a river or an ocean nearby and whether the city is in a valley or on a hill. Now this perspective is there, existing whether or not you are on the top floor to see it. It is up to you to raise yourself up to higher levels and if you do you will have a new perspective.

"The temporal cause of Man is in the past in Time: vertical cause is his meaning, and his meaning will be the level of being to which he belongs." Maurice Nicoll

THE FOUR WAYS

The efforts to reach this level of Being have been defined in different traditions as ways to the developed unity of Will and they correspond to the first three different kinds of Man in the previous diagram of the seven kinds of Man. That is, the way of the physical Man #1, the way of the emotional Man #2, and the way of the intellectual Man #3. However, this esoteric teaching called the Fourth Way is a path to developing unity of '*spiritual will*' and its aim is becoming Man #4.

All esoteric systems begin with the idea that there is something higher than we are. Esoteric teaching says that this "something higher" is within you as a higher, possible and already existing level of yourself, *not yet attained,* that can open up the possibility of receiving higher influences from above that higher level. That is why Christ said: "The Kingdom of Heaven is within you." The Work leads to attaining that higher level of yourself. It has nothing to do with the popular 'New Age' narcissistic idea that you *are* God simply because you are alive. It means exactly what Christ said – this something higher exists "*within you*" and is accessible to you, but is not you as you are. What happens to any individual if they attain this higher level is unknown to us except to say that it comes from another level above them, inaccessible to untransformed mankind.

So, it becomes necessary for you to think in a new way to be able to make contact with this Kingdom of Heaven. *"Be transformed by the renewal of your mind." (Romans 12:2)* The renewal of your mind means acquiring a 'new mind' by thinking in a new way and putting the mind in the right order because right order leads to a unified spiritual will. A unified will means that what is preeminent in you is a singular, individual, stable, and authentic self that possesses qualities not belonging to the changing contradictory wills of the undeveloped self. To start with, the untransformed self has its mind in the wrong order so that as we are we can't even trust ourselves to do something as ordinary as keeping our word or our promises and this is because of our temporary, intermittent will which is not unified or stable.

There are four legitimate 'ways' of developing a permanent unity of 'will': The Way of the Fakir, the Way of the Monk, the Way of the Yogi, and the Fourth Way or the Way of Consciousness. The First Way is the Way of the Fakir which corresponds to Man #1 who, in order to achieve unity of will, develops 'physical will', that is, power over the body, by subjecting the body to the most severe disciplines and even tortures such as holding the arms out to the sides for months and even years at a time. Although this kind of physical discipline can result in the formation of a permanent will it is without understanding since the emotions and intellect are not developed and so is of no use in the world except perhaps as a side show. The Second Way is the Way of the Monk which corresponds to Man #2 and is the path of developing a unified will through the emotional discipline of devotion to faith and religious feelings, and by making religious sacrifices. Only a man with very strong religious emotions can become a 'monk' in the true sense. All his discipline is concentrated on subjecting his emotions to his faith, and in this way he develops unity of will. His body and his mind, however, may remain entirely undeveloped in which case he is of very little use in the world. Developing control of his body and his intellect can only be achieved by making new sacrifices and undergoing new disciplines and hardships. Very few get as far as this. The Third Way is the Way of the Yogi corresponding to Man #3. This is the way of knowledge, the way of the mind. The Yogi develops his mind and control of his thoughts to attain unity of will but he may not be able to make use of the results of his attainment because his body and emotions remain undeveloped.

These are the first three 'ways'. They all have one thing in common which is that from the very beginning practitioners must undergo a complete change of life, a renunciation of all worldly things including family and friends, home and attachments, and go into a monastery or a 'school' in order to attain any unity of will in one of these ways.

The Fourth Way is the way of developing a unified will in and through life. It does not require that a person give up or renounce everything in their life. Since it is *in life* the conditions *of life* which a person occupies are the best possible conditions for him to be in, in order for the Work to find him. They correspond to what he is and any other conditions would be artificial to him. In the Fourth Way it is possible to follow the Work while remaining in the usual conditions of life, maintaining current relationships with people, and without giving up or renouncing anything. The primary demand of the Work is the demand for understanding. A Man must not do anything that he does not understand, except as an experiment under the supervision and direction of a teacher. Faith is not required in the Fourth Way. A man must see for himself the truth of what he is told, and until he is satisfied he must not do anything. The Fourth Way makes it possible to work in the physical, the emotional, the intellectual, and the spiritual parts of a man, all at once, so that when he attains a unified spiritual will he can make good use of it in the world.

In addition to these four 'ways' there are also artificial ways that give only temporary results, and wrong 'ways' that might even give permanent but bad results.

THE FOUR BODIES OF MAN

Corresponding to the four different ways we have the Four Bodies of Man. This subject is a significant central aspect of the Work. The teaching is that Man, living in the given body is capable of developing three further bodies composed of finer energies.

"Man is given by the Universe an organized physical body which works, but not a psychological body." (Maurice Nicoll)

When a child is born it has an organized body that works in an amazing way. The child is born with its heart beating, its blood circulating, with the digestive system ready to work, and many other miraculous features. Then the child grows up and becomes surrounded by personality which means it has acquired a psychological body. But the psychology is not organized, it is in chaos as opposed to the organized physical body. As a result, it can think one thing, feel another and do something completely different without even noticing the contradictions. As we are we have no unified psychological body. Life does not create this unity in us because it is not required by life. It is a luxury. It is only through esoteric teaching and 'work' on ourselves that the formation of an *organized* psychological body becomes possible.

Various teachings using different terminologies describe Man as having four *bodies* all referring to the same structure. In Christian teaching the first body is the physical body, known in Christian terms as the 'carnal' body. The second body in Christian teaching is called the 'natural' body, which may represent the emotional and intellectual functions. The third is the 'spiritual' body. In certain Eastern teachings the four bodies are divided roughly into 'physical', emotional - (feelings and desires), 'mind' and 'will' bodies. In the Fourth Way the first body is the moving/instinctive body. These two make up the physical body. The second body is the emotional body. The third body is the intellectual body. The fourth body is called the will body. The fourth 'will body' is where the potential for spiritual development is located. That development results in a unified spiritual will and evolution becomes possible.

An ordinary person does not possess all of these bodies or their corresponding functions. An ordinary person is governed by their physical body and all the functions of the other bodies are controlled by the physical body which, in turn, is governed by external influences, some from the past which have formed 'habits' and some from the present which we react to in habitual ways. So, as we are, we are controlled by the physical body which is governed by external influences and the next three functions depend on the physical body and the external influences it receives. Feelings and desires, which are the functions of the second body depend upon accidental shocks and influences received by the first, or physical body.

Thinking, which is the function of the third body is an entirely automatic process. And although the emotions and thinking functions are interior to the physical body they are a product of the influences received through the experiences of the physical body, past and present. An ordinary person has no real will body, they have only desires of a greater or lesser degree of duration. And because external influences are accidental and nothing is formed internally, there is nothing that emanates from the individual to control any function. So, nothing truly belongs to the person but is only an automatic response to random external influences.

On the other hand, in a person possessing all four bodies and their corresponding functions, the actions of the physical body depend upon the influences coming from the other three bodies. They originate from the 'will body' which has consciousness and individuality and a single permanent Real 'I', all directed by a unified spiritual will. Real 'I' is 'Master', so instead of randomly stimulated automatic thoughts, thinking is directed by Real 'I' and consciousness issuing from the unified spiritual will body. In the place of the contradictory actions of arbitrary desires, emotions are directed by thinking functions coming from Real 'I'. The actions of the physical body are under the control of the other three bodies because Real 'I' is able to overcome the reluctance and resistance of the physical body.

Only this kind of will can truly be called 'free' because it is independent of external influences. The question is *what* is going to control *what* in an individual? Is it going to be capricious external life that is in control, or consciousness and individuality?

"In a fully developed man – that is, a man possessing individuality, consciousness and will – it is not life and changing outer circumstances that drive him. Such a man has something organized in him that can resist life, something from which he can act. And this is because he possesses more bodies than the one he received at birth." (Maurice Nicoll)

This concept can be represented in the following diagram. The direction of the arrows shows whether the person is governed by the external side or the internal side. Only someone with an organized psychology can be governed from within.

External Man>>>>>>>>>>>>>>>>>>>>Internal Man

Life>	Body	Personality	Psychology- Nothing Organized

External Man<<<<<<<<<<<<<<<<<<<< Internal Man

Life>	Body	Personality	Psychology- Something Organized

If what is more external begins to obey what is more internal, then the internal Man has developed something organized that can control the outer or external Man. The order of things begins to be reversed. The Man is no longer so driven by life and its external influences, by changing circumstances, and by the automatic reactions of his personality to life and the habits of his body. He is no longer driven only from outside, he is no longer a slave of his body, but begins to be controlled from within.

This "something organized" is called a *second body* in this teaching. In that connection let us reflect on the Gospel teaching where Christ says that unless a man is re-born, he cannot enter the Kingdom of Heaven. Birth means a body and rebirth means a second body. When speaking of the resurrection of the dead, Saint Paul says in *(1 Cor. 15:44):*

"It is sown a natural body; it is raised a spiritual body. There is a natural body, and there is a spiritual body."

This Fourth Way teaching is about developing your spiritual body by way of organizing your psychological body. Then you can be reborn in a spiritual body, which has Real 'I', Objective Consciousness, Individuality, Unified Will, and Real Conscience. To make this idea clearer we will look at the diagram of the "Four Bodies of Man" when they are undeveloped and when they are fully developed:

FOUR BODIES OF MAN

Instinctive/Moving Body	Emotional Body	Intellectual Body	Will Body
physical body	emotions	mind	

UNDEVELOPED MAN WORKED BY LIFE INFLUENCES:

Outer>>**Inner**

Fourth Way Terminology:

1st Body	2nd Body	3rd Body	4th Body
physical body worked by external influences	emotions resulting from influences produced in 1st Body	thoughts proceeding from emotions	temporary and contradictory 'wills' created by emotions and thoughts

DEVELOPED MAN OBEYING CONSCIOUSNESS / WILL:

Outer<<<<<<<<<<<<<<<<<<<<<<<<<<<<<<<<<<<<<<<<<**Inner**

1st Body	2nd Body	3rd Body	4th Body
Physical Body obeying thought and emotions subject to Consciousness and Will	Emotional powers and ← desires obeying thought subject to Consciousness and Will	Thinking functions ← obeying Real 'I' Consciousness and Will	Real 'I' Unified Will ←Consciousness Real Conscience Individuality

77

Having these bodies developed means that you are in the *right order* internally.

In the case of the undeveloped person, the accidental arbitrary events and impressions from life influence the body, which influences the emotions, which generate automatic thoughts. A person like this has no real will because 'will' is constantly changing according to ever changing outer events, and external influences.

Man is not born with the finer bodies of the developed Man but they can be cultivated in him given the right conditions. As you can see, in developed Man the inner 4th Body where there is Real 'I' directs the functions of all the other bodies. Real 'I' possesses all of the attributes listed and is under the influence of Higher Mind or the Kingdom of Heaven. Thinking functions are directed by Real 'I', emotions are the result of the thinking functions and the physical body obeys the other three bodies issuing from a unified spiritual will.

However, the resultant 'second body' is not indispensable because the physical body possesses all of the necessary functions for life. The physical body works with the same substances that compose the higher, finer bodies only they are not unified in undeveloped Man, and so do not belong to him. They belong to the influences that control him. The ordinary man has all of the corresponding functions to those of the higher bodies although they are of a very different quality since they are arbitrary and automatic and unstable. As we are, our psychic life changes at every moment with the shifting conditions of external life which means that we are governed by the instability of outer circumstances. This includes our thinking and emotional functions because they are mechanical in action and so beneath the intentional functions of developed man. But these functions can be

78

unified or *fused* into a singularity. The word 'fused' is emphasized because it takes a certain kind of metaphorical heat produced by the psychic friction in a man who struggles within himself, with himself. If he struggles with the thoughts and desires that arise in him automatically, he will create a kind of heat that will gradually transform his inner world into a unified organized singularity.

So, by means of a special kind of *inner work* man can organize and solidify his psychological life through which a unified spiritual will, or Real 'I' is in charge, Objective Consciousness is present, Individuality is manifest, Real Conscience is revealed, and Real Will has the power to *do*. That would mean Man has acquired a second body, a Divine spiritual body, through which he is connected to what is above him.

CENTERS

To continue the teaching on the Four Bodies of Man we need to understand that we have three corresponding centers, one above the other. In this teaching these are arranged in this fashion:

Intellectual Center
Emotional Center
Moving/Instinctive Center

The physical body is the Moving-Instinctive Center because technically these are both necessary for the existence of life and pragmatically speaking their functions are the only criteria needed to define a person as being alive or dead according to medical science. When these functions stop your life has ended. Also, there is no Will Body represented in this part of the teaching because its existence depends on the organization of the Emotional Center and the Intellectual Center. In an unorganized, undeveloped person it exists only as a possibility or at best a 'Divine Spark'. You will notice in the previous diagram that occupying the place of the Will Body in the undeveloped Man are different and contradictory 'wills' of a longer or shorter duration.

The important thing to understand and verify for yourself is that each of these centers has its own kind of intelligence, each different from the others. The Instinctive part of the Moving-Instinctive Center, for example, is very intelligent. It regulates all the systems of the body, calculating and balancing all of interconnected functions from breathing to internal secretions and it does it automatically without you having to think about it. You don't have to think about how to digest your dinner. Digestion happens with all its complicated processes in an automatic way. The Moving part of the Moving-Instinctive Center cooperates with the Instinctive Center on processes like breathing in and out, and keeping your heart beating and blood flowing, but it also has its own intelligence. It is responsible for the multitude of complex calculations involved in moving the muscles so that you can run down the stairs or catch a ball. You might imagine what would happen if you tried to 'think' which muscles to use and at what strength and speed in order to run down the stairs or catch a ball. These two centers function in harmony in a healthy person to give you a physical body. That is why the Work teaches that we are *given* a physical body at birth that is organized and works.

However, the Emotional Center and the Intellectual Center are filled with what we acquire from our life experiences from day one. They are not organized and their functions are constantly interfering with the functions of the other centers.

For example, you could be very anxious about whether or not you would catch that ball and thinking about all of the opinions other people will have if you do or if you don't catch it. This is a common way that the Emotional and Intellectual Centers interfere with other functions. As a result, we often use the wrong center and/or the wrong energies for the task at hand, making us less competent than we could be, and wasting much of our available energy. The Work compares this normal state of a person to a house in disorder; the 'master' is not at home and anyone can enter and occupy it using the master's name.

Individually these two Centers also have very different 'intelligences' that work in very different ways. Your 'feelings' and desires belong to the Emotional Center which is full of self-emotions and negative emotions. The Emotional Center functions are much faster than the Intellectual Center's functions and they have a peculiar quality of power over you. The Emotional Center can perceive the inner state of another person and it can even be clairvoyant when it is purified. Your thoughts belong to the Intellectual Center and work slower than emotions and can be changed more easily. In other words, you can change the way you think easier than you can change the way you feel. But each has its own kind of logic. The Intellectual Center uses reason and logic to 'see' a situation while the Emotional Center can 'feel' a situation.

All of the centers have different kinds of '*minds.*' Each Center is designed for a different purpose and use, also, each is subdivided into higher and lower levels of functioning. We ordinarily only use the lowest parts of our Centers because they require *no attention or effort.* For instance, the lowest part of the Emotional Center is engaged almost entirely with "I like," "I don't like" feelings. It takes the effort of attention to use the higher parts or higher functions of our Centers. Learning something or creating or building something takes attention which means you are using your higher ordinary functions. The higher functions of the Emotional and the Intellectual Centers can hear obscurely a little of what is coming from above. That is why it is so important to understand that these two Centers have to be developed before anything else can happen. Physical practices - that means any moving or instinctive disciplines or exercises - alone won't produce any change in your level of being because you are leaving out the two most important Centers that have to be worked on and changed first of all.

We have then, four kinds of intelligences or conduits of meaning in each of us. Intelligence gives us a relationship to something through meaning. A thought has meaning, an emotion has meaning, a movement has meaning, a sensation has meaning.

Taking note that the Work joins the Moving and Instinctive Centers into one 'mind', that means that we have to understand that we all have three centers with three minds that each relate us to the external and internal worlds differently and that they do not work in harmony. They interfere with each other, hypnotize each other, use each other's functions, and use the wrong energies. This is not a theoretical or unimaginable idea. You can and must verify it for yourself by observing these different centers in action within yourself. For example, if you are doing math in your head, which center is active; if you are cleaning your house, which center is active; if you are angry, which center is active? *To observe which center is at work in you at a particular time is the beginning of practical work on yourself.* This first step must be taken.

The ultimate reason for this practice is because we also have two Higher Centers within us that are continually speaking to us but with a higher vibrational quality which we cannot 'hear' or receive due to the confused, distracted, distorted, loud and coarse functions of our lower centers. We must be able to identify the activities of our different centers so that we can work on them, organize and purify them so that they might be able to hear Higher Centers speaking to us.

"The Work teaches that there are in us, fully developed, two higher centers that are sending their influences down on us continually, only we cannot hear them. These centers communicate with influences coming from higher levels. The object of the Work is to cleanse our lower centers, to clear them out, to open their windows, so that they can begin to transmit these ideas and directions coming from higher centers." Maurice Nicoll

If we reach this stage in our development through Work efforts, then the direction to the next stage of our development and how we are to proceed will be revealed to us. We will have passed under the influences coming down from above and begin to be governed from above instead of from below; from the internal spiritual side instead of the external life side. Growth, evolution, or transformation, depends on getting in touch with these influences coming down from above, from Higher Centers, or the Kingdom of Heaven as it is called in the Gospels. They are fully developed yet we do not even recognize their existence because our level of intelligence is too low to comprehend theirs. For example, if we were to suddenly become conscious in the Higher Mental Center we would be inundated with insights, perceptions and understanding so extraordinary and contradictory to our ordinary state that it would actually be dangerous for our psyche. Therefore, the aim of the Work, put in other words, is to prepare our lower centers, through purification, for the reception of the Higher Centers.

If you constantly feed your lower centers with the ideas of the Work, if you study them, contemplate them, and practice them, then little by little change will become possible, but only through your own inner choice by realizing that you prefer not to be such a slave to your lower self who is your greatest enemy. The Higher centers can only be reached by the purification and organization of the lower centers. This is especially true of the Emotional Center which is filled with the 'dirt' of negative emotions which, practically speaking, makes us deaf. It cannot happen in an artificial way, by externally imitating a 'positive' personality. It can only happen through sincere observation, understanding, and a growing distaste for negative emotions.

The following simple diagram shows the structure of the four lower and two higher intelligences within us:

THE INTELLIGENCE OF CENTERS

Four Ordinary Intelligences

Thought	**Higher Mental Center**
Emotions	**Higher Emotional Center**
Motion	Sensation

The things that keep us stuck in the lowest functions of our ordinary centers are the following: we are hypnotized by

external life and our responses to it; the lower functions
require no attention, no effort; we attribute full consciousness
to ourselves and so don't realize that we are asleep; we aren't
aware that we have a choice to awaken from this sleep and
change the quality of our being; we don't realize our true
position on this Earth or our real meaning for being here; we
choose, without knowing, to remain asleep in the
comfortable, effortless, automatic habits of our physical,
emotional, and mental centers.

A, B, AND C INFLUENCES

The Work teaches that there three kinds of influences that
affect humanity and these are A, B, and C influences. A
influences are created in life by life; by its interests,
commerce, conflicts, ambitions, laws, careers, mass events,
politics and all the personal business of being alive in the
world. They have no relationship at all to B and C influences.
You must be able to free yourself to some extent from A
influences so that you can gradually surrender yourself to the
influences of the Work.

B influences are outside of life influences. They have their
origin in C influences but are translated or altered by life
influences so as to be understood by untransformed Man,
because Mankind's inner destiny, his evolution, does not lie
in life which creates only A influences.

Doing the Work puts you under C influences. C influences
don't originate in life but from outside of life, above life on
earth from the Conscious Circle of Humanity, or the
Kingdom of Heaven. These influences are constantly
speaking to us to convey ideas about awakening and
development, but to a person asleep their language is
incomprehensible. Because it is impossible for the finer

energies of C influences to be received directly into the coarse noisy life of sleeping mankind, life influences alter them into B influences. So, C influences are altered by A influences as they pass into life to produce B influences. They are changed into a language sleeping humanity can receive. The Gospels are a good example of B influences. They originate in C influences but they have been inevitably altered by A influences as they enter into the life of Man.

"Now all the traces in history concerning the idea that man is capable of reaching something of incalculable value, a treasure that cannot be estimated, through inner work on himself, constitute what are called in this system B influences. Since they do not relate to life, their existence in life is inexplicable unless we understand that they are essential for humanity—unless humanity wishes to perish totally in hate and destruction, which is a possibility closer to us than ever before. But if anyone wishes to ask for a clear example of B influences now existing in life, let him take as an example the New Testament, or rather, the four Gospels, which alone contain the teaching of Christ, and let him only take the recorded words of Christ. It will be obvious to him that the ideas contained in these words are not similar to the ideas belonging to A influences—to the newspapers—and are obviously about something different from the ordinary aims and interests of life, although, in a subtle way, they bear on the latter. Let him only reflect that he is taught to struggle with hatred and look into himself and see what he is like.

"To regard one's life as nothing but cause and effect is not to grasp the idea that everyone can come into new causal influences. Otherwise there would be only "Truth" and no "Mercy". This idea is expressed in religious literature as "forgiveness of sins". All transformation depends on the idea that you can be under one set or another set of influences.

*That is one of the central teachings in the Gospels, in
Christ's teaching.... One has to see that on one level of living
there can be only the level of cause and effect belonging to it.
But the Gospels and this Work teach that – if you do this
Work – there is a totally different line of cause and effect,
and a transforming force enters your existence."*
Maurice Nicoll

This is the reason why we work to organize and purify our
lower centers for the reception of our Higher Centers. They
conduct C influences from the Kingdom of Heaven within us
and guide us toward our full development – individual
evolution. The communication coming from the level of
Conscious Circle of Humanity reaches us not in a language
of words that we can learn to decipher but in inspiration,
understanding, guidance and direction.

THE LAW OF THREE

One of the foundational teachings in the Work is called the
Law of Three and it states that in any manifestation there are
always three forces at work. These are called the Active or
First Force, the Passive or Second Force, and the
Neutralizing or Third Force. The Active Force is the force
that initiates. The Passive Force is the force that opposes or
resists whatever the Active Force initiates or proposes. The
Neutralizing Force is sometimes called the reconciling force
because it brings the first two opposing forces into some kind
of relationship that is neither Active or Passive but something
'other' that transcends the opposites bringing them into a
kind of relationship that allows for a manifestation to appear.
This idea can be represented by the following diagram:

Third or Neutralizing Force
*

*   *

First or Active Force ←----------→ Second or Passive Force

First Force and Second Force can never produce a manifestation because they cancel each other out. A Third or reconciling Force is needed to bring them into a relationship that includes both but is neither.

Let's take an ordinary life example. Suppose you want to improve your education. That would be First Force. Whatever opposes your desire to do so – for instance, you have no time to devote to classes, you have no money to pay for them, you're too lazy or too intimidated to try something new - this is Second Force, the force of opposition. If 'life' is Third Force for you any outcome is possible, good or bad, depending on your relationship to life issues. But without Third Force you will keep going back and forth between First and Second Forces with no results.

This is a very mundane example to simply illustrate one way in which these forces act in life. The important point being, that if life is your Third Force then you will always get a certain quality of results, sometimes good, sometimes bad but all belonging to the level of consciousness belonging to the sleep of humanity.

However, if the Work becomes your Third Force then you will be under different influences from a higher level and the quality of manifestation will be at a higher level. For the

Work acting as Third Force means that the Holy Spirit is the reconciling factor and any manifestation will be in harmony with the Kingdom of Heaven. This is our aim in the Work because, after all, what should be your deciding factor in any circumstance? Shouldn't it be God's will and not your own?

In the example given above most life influences would determine that you should increase your education but what if that is the wrong path for you or the wrong path at the time, or maybe you should be doing something else that is more important, or that could lead to your fulfillment. How can you choose from your small perspective what would be the right action? You can't. That's why putting yourself under the Third Force of the Work is the only path to a right resolution. And, to be quite clear, you cannot hear from the Work as Neutralizing Third Force – meaning the reconciling factor of the Holy Spirit – unless you are in some condition of purification. The corruption of negative emotions, for instance, is not a receptive environment conducive to anything Holy. This is why the Work says that we must prepare our ordinary centers for the reception of Higher Centers which is the Kingdom of Heaven within you.

"At the lowest level of creation....there is no Third Force— no "Holy Spirit". Here the opposites are widest apart. They are completely separated. There is no relating force. The most inconceivable extremes ....exist with nothing in between. Nothing harmonizing, nothing of mind, nothing ordered, nothing with meaning, nothing with beauty, nothing of intelligence, nothing of love can exist there. Only horror, meaninglessness, ugliness, shapelessness, mindless cruelty, destruction, dissonance, and mad discord exist. This is HELL. I point this out purposely, because Hell is creeping into everything in this terrible century—even into art, poetry and music, which used to connect us with GREATER MIND.

There is no Third Force in them. Everything is disconnected, unrelated. This is the briefest, most comprehensive formulation—absence of Third Force." Maurice Nicoll

The only way to connect with the Third Force of the Work is by doing the Work of making your personality passive. *"So you will see how absurd a man is if he thinks he can make his Personality passive by himself in his own way while Life is obviously his Neutralizing Force. It simply cannot be done. Only the Work can do it. So, hearing the Work is not enough. You have got to do it. Christ said: "Whoso heareth these words of mine, and does them not, shall be likened unto a foolish man, which built his house upon the sand." (Matthew 12:26) Maurice Nicoll*

ESSENCE

The Work teaches that the most real part of us, the part we are born with, comes down from the stars, from above the level of life on this earth. This is called our *Essence* and it descends into incarnated life from a very high place in the universal scale. Essence is then surrounded by a physical body which is made from the materials obtained from both parents. The body exists in the three-dimensional world but the Essence is different. The body perishes but Essence does not, it is eternal. We cannot see essence but we can grasp the concept. It's why we experience ourselves as ageless whether we are twenty-five or sixty-five regardless of what life events and the aging process have done to us.

When we are born we are nothing but Essence and our given body, however, being born among sleeping people we gradually begin to acquire a Personality which surrounds Essence. This is a *necessary development* because Essence is weak and cannot grow past a certain point because it cannot get the right food. Personality is an external development acquired to enable us to make contact with outer life, do our jobs and live our life in the world. At first Essence is active and gets in contact with the world through the body but as Personality is acquired Essence becomes passive and after a few years it is the Personality that is active and in contact with the world.

"There is the first teaching that Man is of two distinct parts called Essence and Personality. The next thing is that a man is born as Essence only and has no Personality. The third thing is that Essence only grows a little and becomes surrounded by Personality. The next thing is that Essence and Personality are not under the same number of laws (because they are on different levels). *Man, therefore, has two lives possible to him, one belonging to Essence and the other to Personality. The fifth thing is that Personality becomes active and in consequence Essence becomes passive. The personality and its life dominate the Essence which remains undeveloped. The sixth thing is that the object of the Work is to reverse this state in Man and to cause Essence to become active and Personality passive. The seventh thing is that life and the world act as neutralizing or third force to keep Personality active and Essence passive. It is only when the Work becomes neutralizing force that a reversal can take place and Essence become active and Personality passive." Maurice Nicoll*

This means that there are two possible triads in Man. In the first triad Personality is active as First Force and Essence is passive as Second Force and Life is Neutralizing Force. This configuration is necessary and inevitable for mankind and it develops this way in all of us. The other possible triad for man is that Essence is active First Force, Personality is passive Second Force and the Work is Neutralizing Third

Force. Life does not produce this second triad. It is not necessary for a person to live in ordinary life and therefore, it does not just happen. Two things are necessary to produce such a condition in a person. The first is finding a teaching purposefully designed to bring about this new triad in which a new neutralizing force exists. The second thing is for a person to live this teaching and do all that it teaches. Then there are two other conditions necessary required for this transformation to take place. First a person must be willing to take this teaching seriously into their mind and that depends on whether or not their mind is open to anything other than the concerns of external life. Then the person must begin to will and to follow its truth. The person has freedom of choice in both these matters.

"The Work is a mental instrument to connect the human race with Higher Centers. It can be fitted into the mind and if rightly connected up can transform thinking by changing the powers of reception. Now all true esoteric teaching exists because man is asleep and can awaken. That is why the Gospels exist. That is why this Work, which is a reformulation and called sometimes Esoteric Christianity, exists. But a man cannot be persuaded or dazzled by miracles or compelled by force to awaken. He himself can only awaken himself. Only the simplest and, as it were, most innocent, unsophisticated and real side of a man can receive esoteric teaching aright and this is what is meant by "Whosoever shall not receive the Kingdom of God as a little child shall in no wise enter therein." (Luke 18-17). By the little child is meant Essence. Esoteric teaching must reach Essence. Esoteric teaching is always about the "Kingdom of God". It is always about inner development possible to man – namely, the growth of Essence. And Essence cannot grow unless it is fertilized by the "Word of God". I have pointed

out to you often that the Lord's Prayer....says: "Our Father which art in Heaven." It ignores completely the father who provided half the building material for our bodies. It is speaking of Essence, which has no father here." Maurice Nicoll

So, we see that each person is an undeveloped organism made up of inborn Essence which is passive and acquired Personality which is active. Life as Neutralizing Force keeps this dynamic in place unless the Work becomes Neutralizing Force in which case the position of Essence and Personality is reversed. Only esotericism can accomplish this goal, and only through the individual's own choice.

Real inner change is a development of Essence which is the most authentic and deepest part of you. For this change to happen personality must gradually become passive. The true meaning of becoming passive in the Work sense is to become *passive to the reactions of your personality.* This is also the real meaning of detachment. Detachment doesn't mean becoming an inert unresponsive lump without desires or emotions. And it certainly doesn't mean not caring about anything at all. That is psychological pathology. It simply means subjecting all of the reactions of your acquired personality, which includes your will, to God's will. This is something you cannot do unless you understand how and why to make your personality passive. It requires a very active conscious inner state of working on yourself which is a far more difficult task than simply cancelling out your emotions. Passivity in the Work sense leads to inner purity while the wrong practice of detachment leads to mental illness and is a source of vanity which increases and strengthens the personality.

Essence cannot grow by itself beyond a point and it doesn't have the maturity or strength to function in the world beyond that point and that is why personality must be formed around essence to give the individual the means to interact with life in the world. It is the personality that acts, not the individual. The personality enables the person to learn all about the life he is born into, the historical period, and the cultural environment that belongs to his life on earth. The richer the personality the better for the eventual growth of Essence. The more a person knows about the world and how it works, the more education he has, the nicer the personality will be.

So, the personality must go out into life and learn from experience what it is all about and get to the point of realizing that all it has to offer is meaningless to Essence. Then he may begin to long for a return to his origin and if he is fortunate he may begin the return journey back to his 'father' as we see exemplified in the parable of the Prodigal Son. The *descent* of Essence into life necessarily means that a *re-ascent* to its origin is possible. Every living thing longs for an unarticulated reunion with that from which it came. Therefore, if a person comes to the point of realizing that external life does not feed his or her innermost part and seeks a reunion with their original source - the part closest to God - they may be able to strengthen Essence through long inner work and facilitate their reconnection with that source.

However, first we must understand that Essence can only grow through what is true and genuine. It cannot grow through what is false or pseudo. *Lies kill Essence.* Truth develops it. Insincerity or falsehood cannot feed it although they can and do feed the Personality which has life on earth as its origin. Personality being based on self-love is not genuine and cannot love anything higher than itself. It cannot love either its neighbor or God because the self-love always comes first. So, the Personality has to be gradually made passive so that Essence may grow by the truth of this Work.

Every time you make a conscious effort to make the
reactions of your acquired personality passive, the energy
that would have passed into the reactions of personality will
be diverted to the growth and strengthening of Essence. This
diversion is not something you have to conduct. It happens as
a consequence of depriving the Personality of force. Your
part in this equation is only to make the conscious effort of
becoming passive to Personality. As a result of this inner
struggle the action of the Work within you will feed Essence
with the energy that would have gone into Personality.
Although the loss of Personality may temporarily feel
disorienting at first, since you cannot react in your typical
ways, it is ultimately a gain because it strengthens the most
real part of you - your Essence.

A person held by Personality only is not a real person.
Everything he does is insincere including even what appear
to be charitable acts. This is because the Personality only acts
from some kind of self-interest, whether it's a feeling of
merit or for praise, it is pseudo, not the real person acting. If
a person is not held by something deeper than Personality
they are not a real person at all and are not capable of
individual evolution. They are the psychologically dead that
Christ referred to when he said "let the dead bury the dead."
A person in this condition may appear to be very successful
and have a strong personality in the world. Yet they are dead
in the sense that they are completely cut off from Essence
and unable to develop internally.

So, Essence can only grow at the expense of Personality
which is why the Work is directed at the Personality. You
cannot work on Essence directly but only by making
Personality passive, by working against the features of
Personality which are purely acquired psychological
formations in you. Acquiring this Personality that you take as

yourself is called the *first education*, and although it is
necessary it is not all that is available to Man. The Work is a
second education for those who are not fulfilled by the
satisfactions of life.

Making these kinds of efforts leads to the new triad in a
person.

*"This new arrangement is a reversal of the former
arrangement. A reversal of sign has taken place. It begins
when Work in a man begins to become stronger than life.
And this means that something organized has been made in a
man that controls him. For the Work, coming from Conscious
Influences, can form in suitable soil, a receptive organ
through which a man can receive force – that is, his "daily
bread". And since Essence is the most real part of a man and
personality relatively unreal, for this organ to form itself
aright, it must eventually form itself out of what is most real
and sincere in a man. It cannot form itself in the external
man, nor in the hypocrite in a man which is the False
Personality."* Maurice Nicoll

Personality is developed by life but the reason life cannot
develop Essence is because life cannot provide the right kind
of food from which Essence can grow. Essence, which has a
very high origin and is said to "come from the stars," stops
growing at a very young age because life doesn't feed it the
right kind of food. Essence and Personality are on different
levels in vertical scale and so require different kinds of truths
to grow by. But a person who fills his mind with this Work
and its ideas and thinks about them deeply, perceiving their
truth and depths, and acknowledges them and applies them to
himself, is feeding his Essence with the right food and it will
grow. Only the kind of truth that the Work teaches can make
Essence grow. Willing to do the truth of it gives Essence the
right food it came down to receive. Just as the body requires

food and drink to survive so does the Essence require the two foods of *good and truth* that the Work can supply.

"The idea that Personality has to be made passive throughout life, and little by little, before inner development can reach any perfection, is one of the Great Ideas taught by the Work." Maurice Nicoll

Essence is the point from which the real person can grow but it can't do so as long as Personality is active and controls the Inner life. You can't retain your full-blown Personality and develop Essence at the same time. So, all practical work is aimed at gradually making Personality passive so that Essence can become active and a new triad is formed with the Work as Neutralizing Force. That means the Holy Spirit becomes the Reconciling Force, or Third Force in your life which expresses the concept that the *universe is a response to request*. Your personal work efforts are the request through which you lift yourself up and make yourself able to receive a response.

"It is apparent that the development of Essence is a return journey or ascent.... Since it came down from a high level." Maurice Nicoll

PERSONALITY

Since the dynamic between Essence and Personality is so central to the Work it makes understanding Personality in general and your personality in particular extremely important. The study of your own personality will last your lifetime and get deeper as your consciousness expands, but, of course, that is a matter of your own personal work and will vary from one individual to another. However, the study of Personality in general is an extensive undertaking and applies to all of us because we are all under the same laws regarding Personality.

To begin with, as was said, we are born with Essence only, that is, without Personality, however Essence has character and purpose. The acquisition of a personality will affect these factors. Remember that Personality is a necessary development and not to be despised, just purified. If, for instance, you have learned to be a good baker, that is part of your acquired Personality but nothing you necessarily need to get rid of.

Now if you get it into your mind that you're the greatest baker that ever lived, then you have a problem in your Personality that you will have to deal with, but it isn't about baking. The important point here is in discernment and only inner observation will help you with that. However, what we need to grasp is that Personality must grow around Essence to protect it and as a consequence Personality becomes the means through which we interact with the world we are born into. By the age of three or four or five a small child has Personality as the active part of their Being and Essence has become passive. Life, acting on the child has become Third force.

We acquire Personality from the day of our birth through our experiences and the influences in our life. We are, of course, influenced by our parents, and we are also influenced by our home life and siblings, by our culture, ethnicity, religion, and the historic time period we are born into. We are influenced by our community, our education, our peers and teachers, our friends and enemies, and our interests. We are influenced by literature and film, by popular cultural norms and values, and in this age by media venues and collective movements. We react to all of these influences, imitating some, rejecting some, accepting others, and we do this all unconsciously. Many things that have had a profound influence on the formation of our Personality are unknown to us and can never be known. The outcome is that *we are made up of reactions to things we had no control over and did not consent to.*

From all of these influences, imitations and reactions we have formed opinions, attitudes, habits, judgements, perspectives, and a certainty that we are right in all of these things. This is how we *acquire* our Personality.

Personality is based primarily on self-love and it cannot be otherwise. But there is a great danger in mixing self-love with your inner relation to the Work. They are on two different levels which are discontinuous and can never be anything but in opposition to each other. Love of the Work and valuation for it must come before self-love and not be infected by it because you cannot be on two levels at the same time and self-love will ruin your aims in the Work because it always desires to be first.

"To seek to be first, to seek to be the greatest, the most highly placed, is regarded as normal ambition. All this is based on the self-love which dominates our life relations. Life as Third Force in the Life-triad seems, psychologically, to be mainly the self-love. One can then write the Life-triad as Personality Active, Essence Passive and Self-Love Neutralizing Force. From this we can see that the Third or Neutralizing Force of the Work triad cannot be self-love.

"In one of the Epistles Paul speaks of the difficulty he has with people in his groups who do not really care for what he is teaching in itself, but come for other reasons. He says, "they all seek their own" (Phil.2:21). In another place (2 Tim. 3:7) where he is speaking openly of "lovers of self," he says they are "ever learning and never able to come to the knowledge of truth."

99

He means that having only self-love and no love for his teaching they cannot raise their level enough to perceive internally the truth of what he taught and know it for themselves." Maurice Nicoll

Self-love is often hard to discern in the beginning of your personal work but it is an enormous stumbling block. With some verified experience you will come to notice a great difference in inner taste between self-love and love of the Work. There are elements of gratitude, humility and of joyful surrender in love of the Work which are not present in self-love. Try to see self-love or even just self-interest behind all of the manifestations of Personality. And have a new understanding of what Christ meant when He said, *"If any man desire to be first, the same shall be last of all, and servant of all."* (Mark 9:35)

"We are told somewhere in Scripture that unless a man hates himself he cannot understand the teaching of Christ....Christ said : "If any man cometh unto me, and hateth not.... his own life also, he cannot be my disciple. In the Greek, the word translated "one's own life" means "soul" or "psyche". For example, the phrase "to lay down one's life for one's friends" should be translated "to go against one's own soul for the sake of one's friends." We can understand that going against one's soul is equivalent to going against one's self-love and that to hate one's life is to hate this oneself that is formed and controlled by the self-love. We can conceive the soul at our level as a point of intense self-love through which we are made to identify most powerfully. When it is interfered with, we hate." Maurice Nicoll

One of the most significant aspects of our personality is that we truly believe that we have one unchanging I, and full consciousness; that we are aware of all that we say and do and feel and that we do it all intentionally. In the Work this is called Imaginary 'I' because all that it believes is an *illusion* built by imagination. It is the illusion of sleeping humanity and it must be seen through before any change can happen. If you take everything you think, say, feel and do as one unified I, how can you change? You can't. There is no room for movement in a solid thing and no options for change. It is fixed. Through directed observation you will come to see for yourself that this thing you call 'I' is no more than the acquired personality that imagines it is one thing acting all the time in spite of the mighty contradictions of ever changing moods.

In reality you are in Second State, sleep walking through your life using habits of thought, habits of feeling, habitual attitudes, opinions, gestures, words,
and actions which all happen mechanically, without effort. You will observe that it is your personality that acts and not always as you would like it to act. You will recognize that you are not conscious of all that you say, think, feel and do, and often these things happen automatically and unintentionally. And you will observe and verify that there is no unity of 'I' in you. You can think and believe one thing one moment and think and believe the opposite the next, and the same inconsistency is true of your feelings and actions. Yet you call it all 'I'.   *Imaginary 'I'* is what makes this illusion possible. And it must change if you want to change. Always remember that you can't change and stay the same. Sometimes, in times of great danger, serious illness, or brokenness the personality ceases to exist temporarily showing you that you are not 'that'. It is important to note these moments and remember them to reference the fact that you exist even without the personality you know and think of as yourself, and to value that fact.

There is a further development of personality that the Work calls False Personality. Now all personality is false in regard to the fact that you are not born with it, it is acquired. But False Personality is more intensely artificial in that it goes beyond just the required adjustment to life for the purpose of functioning in life. False Personality is adopted to express particular kinds of attributes for the purpose of creating a specific kind of impression. For example, a doctor has his 'doctor' False Personality that is different from his normal acquired personality and might contain aspects of superiority, authoritarianism, presumption of a high valuation, and condescension, among other possibilities.

A drill sergeant has his professional False Personality as well, and a waitress, a salesman, a doorman, an actress, a politician, a librarian, etc. But we also see these kinds of affectations in ordinary people who have adopted personality traits that are meant to define them in desired ways to produce desired perceptions. This is an observable phenomenon in popular and cultural expressions of mannerisms, values and clothing, and also in physical posture, in fashion and language, and collective behaviors. The point here is that False Personality is more deliberately cultivated by the individual, although not wholly consciously, to make a particular impression. And the problem is that it is entrenched in the perception they have of themselves and intractable because the individual actually imagines that it expresses who they are, their Real 'I', when nothing could be farther from the truth.

These kinds of False Personalities are another layer of artifice whose mere construct puts them farther away from the deeper real self.

False Personality is based entirely on imagination and vanity. When you see its manifestations it's sometimes hard to figure out how any reason for vanity could be so obviously absent in constructing an identity but vanity isn't only about physical beauty.

People are vain about their imagined importance, about their intellect or talents, about their affiliations and ethnicity, about presumed superiority for any number of reasons, about their position, their wealth, status, education, ancestry, accomplishments, and simply about their perceived individuality. A very homely person who has gone to the trouble of making themselves even more outlandishly unattractive may be the vainest person you will ever meet. They are vain about their 'difference' and want to make sure everyone notices that difference. Vanity is a master manipulator that makes people say and do all kinds of artificial things that obscure the deeper more authentic person. This degree of vanity in partnership with imagination produces a posturing, posing, insincere, presumptuous, artificial, pseudo-self with a particularly brittle nature. You can be sure that there is nothing authentic to connect with in a person with an outrageous False Personality.

These manifestations of False Personality all belong to what the Work calls Imaginary 'I'. They are *illusions* built out of vanity and imagination. Besides the more observable characteristic traits already mentioned, False Personality attributes to itself an abundance of qualities that it does not possess like moral superiority, individuality, elevated worthiness, special gifts and talents. All of these reasons are why False Personality is
one of your greatest foes, your most vicious adversary, if you are pursuing the path of the Work which leads to authentic humility. Imaginary 'I' and False Personality must slowly die in this process and they will not do so without a fierce struggle for their continued existence. They are who you

think you are and that person must necessarily change as you discover who you really are as you move towards your Real 'I'. Real 'I' lies above you, above the acquired Personality, Imaginary 'I', the False Personality and its affectations, at the third level of consciousness.

"....realizing that the Gospels are not just about "being good" or looking pious or humble or living in poverty or being poor in spirit. They are instructions about how to make Essence active so that it can grow and make contact at a higher level with Real 'I'. The aim is contact – not being good. Gurdjieff said that behind Real 'I' lies God." Maurice Nicoll

These two - False Personality and Imaginary 'I' - can only be recognized through the self-knowledge that comes from the practice of *Self-Observation*. That is why the practical Work begins with the observation of yourself. The illusions we all have about ourselves can only be weakened by seeing them. We cannot change what we do not see. *"Through the gradual wasting of the Personality, through withdrawing energy from its mechanical reactions, which makes it passive, the Essence develops." Maurice Nicoll*
So, try to notice your artificial ways, your affectations, your insincerity, the authenticity of your manners, how you pretend to know what you do not know, and how you act so charming. Then notice how you are a slave to your False Personality having to buy things and do things and say what it wishes to say and not what *you* wish to say. The Work is designed to free you from all of this falsity and the wrong ideas you have about yourself. When you have become free from what does not belong to you and what you have acquired, the feeling of liberation that results is the ultimate feeling of relaxation because you have been released *"from your False Personality which means all of the façade of*

pretense that you are always living by which conducts to you absolutely wrong experiences and makes you get involved in things that do not belong to the path of your essential life."
Maurice Nicoll

It is only through long and very sincere self-observation in the light of what the Work teaches that you can gradually lose these layers of acquired artifice and begin to know what inner peace means. You can't move toward anything more real in yourselves unless you remove these outer layers one by one. But by doing all the Work teaches on its practical side you can move towards this inner thing called Real 'I'. Remembering always to start with changing yourself. That is what was meant when Christ said, *"Thou hypocrite, first of all get rid of the beam in thine own eye."*

So, the first stage of a person is in infancy when personality has not yet developed enough to be active. The second stage is when the person passes into and under life influences where they develop a Personality. The third stage is when a person comes to the point of feeling empty since Personality no longer satisfies them and they want to find new meaning for their existence. Then they are entering this third stage which is defined by Christ when He says to the rich man, *"Go, sell that thou hast, and give to the poor."* The Gospels have nothing to do with ordinary life. They are about this third stage when a new growth of Essence can take place at the expense of Personality. The "poor" in us is the poor development of Essence, and the "rich man" is the Personality.

You are each attached to a complicated mechanism of Personality that takes charge of you at every moment giving you the same thoughts, the same feelings and the same ways of taking life events. This acquired machine of Personality works *mechanically*, automatically, without thought or effort.

However, *you are not this machine.* It is your Personality that reacts mechanically and this is what you have to observe in yourselves. You have to begin to *verify your mechanicalness* through observation according to the Work teaching so that you can see that *It* does, *It* reacts, you do not. And then you must learn to say *"This is not 'I'"* to the mechanical manifestations of Personality. In part, this is how you can make Personality passive.

The realization of the mechanicalness of your Personality is a definite stage in the Work and of great significance because a person cannot change unless they become aware of their mechanicalness.

PICTURES AND IMAGINATION

Another function of this very powerful force in us called imagination is making 'pictures' of ourselves that we carry around with us as part of our False Personality. When a person has a picture of themselves the picture will prevent them from seeing anything that does not correspond to the picture. That effectively keeps them stuck in False Personality which can never approach Higher Centers. If, for instance, you have a picture of yourself as being a very honest person you will never notice how often you lie, or what you lie about, or how you lie – like pretending you know when you do not know or pretending to care when you do not care, or agreeing when you do not really agree. No matter how much you lie you will not see it. The picture you have of yourself obstructs your inner vision. The real person stands behind all of these pictures but never stands *in* his or her picture. However, if you can accept the truth of its imaginary quality then in the case of lying *"this inner confession, this giving way, this*

surrender,.....this giving up of what you have always known to
be a liar in you, is one of the most blessed experiences you
can have in this Work." Maurice Nicoll

Now we all have many imaginary pictures of ourselves but
they all must be seen through and eventually vanish if we
want to move toward Real 'I'.

"What is genuine and what is imaginary can never meet.
They are two different orders of experience on different
planes." Maurice Nicoll

However, it is very difficult to observe imagination because
as soon as you try to observe it, it stops. You may have a
picture of yourself as being a nice person or even a good
Christian. If you do you will never notice how often you
judge other people and feel superior to them. You will not be
aware of how often you criticize others or how you complain
or how you are selfish, and you will always justify your
anger and irritability. You will only be aware of the good
deeds you do and the fact that that you attend church and
tithe and have been baptized.

Whatever picture you have of yourself you can be sure that
you are not at all like that picture. If you think you are a
tough guy, you are actually the weakest of men hiding behind
that picture. If you think you are 'special' you can join the
ranks of everyone else, because everyone thinks they're
special. It is possible, though, to observe the pictures you
have of yourself in retrospect by recalling how they manifest
in posture, movement, facial expression and intonation, in
what you said and what attitude you had. Each picture is
connected with a typical line of fantasy you have about
yourself but through the special Work memories you will
develop over time, you will realize that every picture you
have of yourself is false.

Pictures are made out of imagination and are another part of False Personality which must be struggled against all your life. The more you go with False Personality, which leads the way with what the Work calls the two giants of *Pride* and *Vanity*, the less truth there is in what you do and the more distant you become from Essence which can only grow through what is true and what is good. However, if you increase your consciousness and thereby can *stand behind the façade of your False Personality* you can see through the pictures you have of yourself, and if you acknowledge to yourself what you see, you will remember it.

"If you can begin to see a picture, if you become conscious of it, if you begin to dislike it, if you try to get away from it, to separate from its hypnotic power, if you begin to see that you are not at all like that picture, then the change that results will be exactly what you need. You will fit into what has always been waiting for you, and what you went out of long ago as a child." Maurice Nicoll

The general task then is to make Personality more and more passive through applying the practical side of the Work to yourself. You are all in the prison of your personalities and they use up all of your energies. It is said in this Work that in order to escape from prison that a man must first awaken to the fact that he is in a prison. Self-Observation, as the Work teaches it, will show you the prison of your Personality, and especially your False Personality which is its leading 'devil'. If you use this Work as a guide you will soon see what you have to work on in yourself to make your Personality passive. Then you can apply its practices to what you have observed and all of the energy that would have gone into Personality can go into the growth of Essence.

"I shall always remember the great and joyful sense of freedom that I experienced when I suddenly, at a meeting,

*realized what the Work saying 'You must not react' might
mean to me and my life. Life could be transformed. I was no
longer at the mercy of life. I had found a way to deal with
life.*
*I need not react. No one and nothing could hurt me or even
touch me if I could find the strength not to react. The solution
of the difficulty lay with me. I had the power, if I could learn
to use it, to make life harmless to me. Life was not the master.
I could overcome the difficulties and the unhappiness of life
by becoming passive to them, not reacting to them." Maurice
Nicoll*

A cautionary note: *"Some people of weak being, of weak
knowledge, with no magnetic center, cannot awaken from the
deep sleep they are in. They cannot awaken from False
Personality in themselves and if you are so foolish as to try to
awaken them from their sleep you will only be hated by
them." Maurice Nicoll*

THE DOCTRINE OF 'I's

In regard to the personality and all of its constant inner and
outer chatter we can recognize the functions of the three
centers – Moving-Instinctive, Emotional, and Intellectual. It
must be understood that each center affects the other centers.
Sensations evoke emotions and thoughts; emotions evoke
thoughts and sensations; thoughts evoke emotions, sensations
and actions.
These functions all overlap and interfere with one another
and they are all generated by habits of the acquired
personality. Its features are constantly reacting for you, in
your name, without consulting your Real 'I'.

These individual psychic events are called *I's* in the Work because we say 'I' to them, we invest in them our belief that they are our singular Real 'I' speaking. For example: I think …., I imagine…., I presume…., I was taught…., I know…., are all 'I' belonging to the Intellectual Center as are countless more. The Emotional Center has 'I's that are always engaged in self-emotions and many of them speak like this: I like, I don't like, I want, I don't want, I feel, I don't feel, I love, I hate, I'm happy, I'm sad, I'm angry, I'm bad, I'm good….and the list could go on almost forever. The Moving-Instinctive Center will have these kinds of 'I's: I'm cold, I'd like to go for a run, I need to take a nap, I want to work on my project, I'd like to sit here indefinitely without moving, I want something to eat, I couldn't take another bite, well, maybe just one.

Now when you say 'I' to something you invest your 'self' in it without realizing that it is just one of many possible 'I's within you. You give it your force and identity and belief that it is the one unalterable 'I' of your true self. This is called *Identifying with yourself* in the Work and it is the most difficult inner condition to become passive to and to overcome.

When you begin to practice Self-Observation, in trying to see which center is active you will notice how often these different 'I's each speak in turn with the presumption that each holds permanent dominion over all the other 'I's. That is, each speaks as if it is 'Master', and you allow it to use your name. Then another 'I' takes its place with the same presumption and you give it the sanction of yourself again by saying 'I' to it even if is in direct contradiction to the last one, i.e., "I have to have a cookie," "I don't want to have a cookie because I'm dieting." As you begin to observe these

110

different 'I's you will start to verify one of the most difficult esoteric teachings about mankind:

MAN IS NOT A UNITY BUT A MULTIPLICITY

This is hard to understand at first and most people find the idea quite offensive. We take ourselves for granted. Without giving it any thought we presume that we are a unified being already just as we presume that we have full consciousness and can do whatever we decide to do and change ourselves with the power of our will. It is quite disconcerting to consider that this is all an illusion but it takes only a little sincere observation to see for yourself that it is so. *Man is Legion.*

"Owing to the multiplicity of one's being it is very difficult to know, to feel, what one is." Maurice Nicoll

You have *acquired* all of these many 'I's in your personality by way of your life experiences, their influences on you, and your reactions to them. Many influences you have no knowledge of. Most were created without your consent, all without your awareness. They belong to your acquired psychology but *they are not you,* they are not your Real *'I'.*

The danger here is expressed in the parable in the Gospel about the sower and the seed. *"The sower went forth to sow his seed: and as he sowed, some fell by the wayside; and it was trodden under foot, and the birds of heaven devoured it...."* When Christ interpreted this parable to His disciples He said; *"The seed is the word of God. And those by the wayside are they who have heard; then cometh the devil, and taketh away the word from their heart, that they may not believe and be saved."* It means that the ideas of the Work fall in the midst of the commotion in one's mind, among the ordinary multiplicity of everyday 'I's. This is the mechanical side of the mind which Christ calls the devil because *mechanicalness is the devil* and it is made up of the legion of 'I's which constitute the mechanics of Man's multiplicity. The point He is making here is that the ideas of the Work must not be taken on the ordinary level of life 'I's or they will be lost in the traffic of Man's multiplicity and "trodden under foot." They are on a higher level than life 'I's and must have their own special place apart from ordinary ideas.

Now, this idea of multiplicity is tremendously offensive because all people believe they have one mind with one permanent, unchanging 'I' which deals with everything, that they have one will, that they possess full consciousness, self-knowledge, and the power to do. This is the greatest illusion. This perspective about oneself is not only wrong it will effectively make any transformation impossible because if you were a unified 'one', a singularity, there would be no possibility of adaptation in order to change. You would not be able to choose one 'I' over another 'I' if everything was one single 'I'. The truth of the matter is that all of your many 'I's exist under the umbrella of *Imaginary 'I'*. They hide their hordes of multiplicity under the illusion of unity that Imaginary 'I' provides.

"It takes so long before people can bear to realize that internally they are not one but many, that they are not a unity and harmony but a multiplicity and disharmony, that they have not one permanent and real 'I' but hundreds of different and quite contradictory 'I's that take charge of them at different moments, that they have no real will but a host of changing conflicting wills, belonging to each of these 'I's, that only rarely do they have moments of consciousness but usually are in a

*peculiar state of waking-sleep, and that as a result of all this
they have no real power of doing and so they live in a world
where everything happens and no one can prevent it from
happening. Even the idea that a man has not one mind but
different centers or minds can be resented or regarded as
being fantastic as is the saying that people are not conscious.
No one in fact will face himself and his real situation."*
Maurice Nicoll

Fortunately, these are facts that can be verified and it
makes sense really, because otherwise how could you choose
the good 'I's and eliminate the bad 'I's as you try to lift your
Being to a higher level? How could you choose which 'I's to
go with and which to ignore, which to nurture and which to
starve, which to value and which to discard in the process of
transformation? How, in fact, could one 'I' rule over another
'I' if you didn't have multiple 'I's in you of different
qualities at different levels.

You already have higher and lower 'I's within you and if
you do not separate your real self from the acquired self you
will always be attributing everything to the self of many 'I's,
that is, your personality. You will attribute your most evil
thoughts and feelings to yourself and you will attribute your
good thoughts to yourself - both disturbing and dangerous
beliefs. But you can be liberated from this illusion and as a
consequence you will have the power to choose not to go
with just any 'I' that comes along, not to believe them, not
give them your permission to speak for you, not to listen to
them, not to argue with them, not to say 'I' to them.
This is how you free yourself from the artificial self that you
have always taken yourself to be. It is how you can eliminate
the 'I's that are silly or useless or harmful to you and choose
the better 'I's and in the process, change your level of Being.
Just as a gardener has to choose what plants to pull out of his

garden patch and which ones to water and fertilize if he wants his garden to flower and produce food, so must we discern what is harmful and useless in our psychology so that we can choose what to nurture. *This is how we make personality passive.*

Understand that you have acquired many things, many habits of thought, feeling and action, many typical reactions to life, and all of these built up *reactions* are usually taken by you as you, yourself. But the Real 'I' in you is not all these things that you keep taking as yourself. There is no such thing as a unified, permanent 'I' in you regardless of what you imagine, and if you don't observe that you have many different 'I's, no change is possible.

"The word 'I' will come out of your mouth at every moment but you will not see that it is a different 'I' speaking at every moment. One 'I' will shout, another 'I' will speak tenderly, and so on. Yet you do not see that each 'I' is utterly different. It is a great shock to self-conceit to realize that there is no such person as 'I'.

But unless this begins to dawn on you, you will never be able to begin to be passive to yourself. You cannot begin to be passive to yourself unless you see yourself as many different people by inner observation and learn about your different 'I's and know especially which 'I's in you that you must never allow to take full charge of you." Maurice Nicoll

It must be emphasized here that the *Doctrine of 'I's* is the most important part of the psychological teaching of the Work. It is the key teaching that begins to make change of yourself possible. If a person cannot see that they are not one but many, they can never separate themselves from the illusion of unity that the sleeping self of many 'I's believes in. You then extend your will to each 'I' and they become the same as yourself, and so they work in you as yourself, and you believe them. You cannot separate yourself from an 'I' if you remain convinced that you are one with it. And taking everything as 'I' will make change impossible because all of your 'I's will hide behind the cloak of illusion called Imaginary 'I' and continue to live inside you. You will not be able to distinguish between one or another 'I' because you remain united with them, taking them all as yourself instead of separate 'I's in you.

Now, as you begin to practice Self-Observation and you begin to see different 'I's in you, you then can say to them "This is not 'I'" and in this way, you take the feeling of *self* out of the 'I' you have observed, and over time, with repeated efforts, that particular 'I' will fade. You are not feeding it with the force of identification so it will diminish and the force you save will pass into the growth of Essence.

"There are many dangerous and harmful 'I's that hover on the edges of your consciousness so that you don't see what they are up to. They act in a silent, subtle way accumulating resentments and harboring negativity that will eventually explode in a reaction that will damage you. Your area of consciousness must be expanding continually until you can see these 'I's and nullify their actions. However, if you take yourself as one you will not be able to practice Self-Observation and will remain under the tyranny of any 'I' that takes charge of you at any moment." Maurice Nicoll

Since this psychological configuration of multiplicity is the same in everyone it is a grave mistake to think that you yourself or anyone else has one permanent unchanging 'I'. You are constantly changing and so is everyone else, although if another person is called David then you both might assume that he is always the same David, when this is quite untrue. To assume that another person is one and the same at all times is to do violence to him or her just as it is to do violence to yourself to think that you are always one 'I'. Both of you have a multitude of 'I's that belong to your personalities. When you have observed this in yourself you will not be able to judge others so easily. But as long as you take yourself as one permanent 'I' you will judge others by thinking that they also have one permanent 'I' and you will not be able to forgive them. Once you begin to verify for yourself that you are full of contradictory 'I's, some good, some bad, this understanding will enable you to be more merciful to others and less judgmental.

"The whole point is to pray for the Neutralizing Force of the Work, which comes only through self-observation and then you can forgive others and be more at peace." Maurice Nicoll

CONSCIENCE AND BUFFERS

The Work teaches that we have two different kinds of conscience. One is our acquired or learned conscience which is the product of our upbringing, culture, country and historical time period, among other things. This includes our social conscience, as well. What we do in polite society may be different than what we do in private but both are based on acquired conscience.

The Objective Conscience of Conscious Man numbers 5, 6, and 7 is quite different from acquired conscience but it is the same in all people of developed consciousness throughout history. Conscious mankind all understand life in all of its aspects in the same way and consequently they understand each other. Every one of us also has this level of conscience within us but it is buried under the learned conscience of our acquired personality. The Work calls this *Buried Conscience.* It is the same in every living person in the world and the

Work, rightly applied, will eventually reveal it. It evolves
with consciousness and can't be separated from it. It is Real
Conscience and is an attribute of evolved Consciousness just
like Real 'I', Real Will, and Individuality. But, as we are we
don't know Objective Conscience, we have only acquired
and Buried Conscience.

Acquired conscience varies in individuals and cultures and
can include everything from dietary issues to outright
murder, theft, lying, and many other actions that would
violate Buried Real Conscience. You can verify for yourself
through observation how your own conscience changes in
different circumstances. In this regard there are two factors
that help keep you asleep to the contradictions in your
conscience and your actions. One is Self-Justifying which
means always putting yourself in the right. The other is an
artificial adaptation called Buffers.

Buffers are a psychological faculty acquired unconsciously
over time in early childhood to lessen the impact of the shock
between contradictions in your personality just like fenders
on a car lessen the shock of a collision. Buffers prevent you
from feeling Real Conscience and make life easier to bear,
but they also prevent you from developing. Without them
you would go mad.

*"What especially prevents a man from seeing
contradictions in himself are buffers. In place of having Real
Conscience a man has Artificial Conscience and buffers.
Behind everyone there stand years and years of a wrong and
stupid life, of indulgence in every kind of weakness, of sleep,
of ignorance, of pretense, of lack of effort, of drifting, of
shutting one's eyes, of striving to avoid unpleasant facts, of
constant lying to oneself, of abuse and blaming of others, of
fault finding, of self-justifying, of emptiness, of wrong talking,
and so on. As a result the human machine is dirty and works*

117

wrongly. Not only this, but artificial appliances have been created in it due to its wrong way of working. And however a person may wish to wake up and become another person and lead another life these artificial appliances interfere very much with his good intentions. They are called Buffers. Like contrivances on railway carriages, their action is to lessen the shock of collision. But in the case of buffers in man their action is to prevent two contradictory sides of himself from coming into consciousness together." Maurice Nicoll

The problem is that only the shock of realizing something about yourself can lead to inner development and the presence of buffers will prevent these shocks and therefore prevent you from developing. In order to break up a buffer it is necessary to see both contradictory sides of yourself that are separated by the buffer at the same time. Once it has been broken up it cannot form again. To have Real Conscience you must see the action of buffers.

We live in a state dominated by self-emotions that we are unaware of due to the action of buffers and this subjective state keeps us from being able to appropriately "love our neighbors". These self-emotions like self-admiration, self-complacency, self-righteousness, self-esteem, self-merit, self-worship, and self-liking, completely distort our memory and because of the presence of buffers keep us unaware of any contradictions. Buffers and self-justifying prevent us from ever seeing that we are wrong and allow us to continue to like ourselves no matter how badly we have behaved. However, no one can ever grow spiritually or psychologically unless their self-liking is disturbed through the practice of self-observation which will create a conscious memory.

IMPRESSIONS

The Work teaches that the human machine needs three different kinds of 'foods' to survive. The first is ordinary food that we ingest. The second is 'air'. The third is Impressions. We can easily understand the body's need for the food we eat but the idea that 'air' is food only makes sense when you consider how it works in the body and that we cannot survive without it. To consider Impressions as 'food' we first have to understand what is meant by the term.

Impressions are mostly psychological in nature although they are generated by external factors and events and our sleeping responses to them as well as our ordinary psychological condition. We receive Impressions from what we see and hear and read among other things. We see a stray puppy and we get an Impression from that image. We hear that we are getting a raise in pay, or that we are going to be fired and we get other Impressions from that information. We read that a friend has died or that our numbers have won the lottery and we get Impressions from that knowledge. When we
are asleep we get Impressions from our dreams, from our comfort or discomfort, from our breathing, our heartbeat, and body temperature. Impressions are the highest food, of the finest materiality, that we receive and so have the most potent impact on us and are, therefore, the most important food of all the foods needed by us.

Ordinary food that we eat is the coarsest food for our bodies. It undergoes several stages of digestion before it becomes fine enough to be used for the functions of life. A piece of meat, for instance, has to be transformed in the digestive system into very fine matter before it can become the energy that can be used for thinking. Similarly, air has to be 'digested' or transformed in the lungs where some parts are selected and some rejected before it can pass into the bloodstream and feed the cells oxygen. Impressions also have to be digested in order to be used by the human machine. However, Impressions coming from the external world usually fall on the acquired Personality and are 'digested' by it in the habitual ways belonging to the machinery of Personality and so always produce the same effects.

If Impressions could fall directly on Essence everything would take on a new, fresh, richer quality and Essence would grow. But one condition that is necessary for Impressions to fall on Essence is that we must be living more in the actual moment when they are received. If we are living in imagination or in the past or in the sleep of personality with all of its habits and associations this will be impossible.

"If you cannot observe how you react, then, of course, nothing can be changed. If you cannot or will not take in any new ideas, again, nothing can be changed. If you think that you can retain your former ways of thinking and feeling and estimating things and simply add something new to yourself as you are, then again you cannot change. It is you that has to change and you are just how you mechanically think and feel about everything. Have you then begun to observe this you, this person who thinks, feels and acts as always? Are you satisfied with this acquired you?" Maurice Nicoll

Your reactions to Impressions are part of your acquired habitual mechanics that must be observed. Since Impressions are our most important food that means that we live by them. We can live a few weeks without food, a few minutes without air, but the Work teaches that if we were deprived of all impressions we would die immediately. This may sound absurd until you think deeply about it.

"No matter what a depressed person eats with his mouth, or what air he breathes, it will not cure him until he gets that letter that he is waiting for in which it is said that he has passed his examination, or that somebody loves him, or that he has won his law suit." Maurice Nicoll

Take a moment to reflect on this. People actually die from depression and heartbreak all of the time, and these conditions are the product of Impressions.

Being exposed to constant bad news, or criticism by others, or continuous faultfinding, form a quality of Impressions that won't give the right conditions for living a normal life. Often, however we tend to try to get favorable Impressions of ourselves from others which is really only to satisfy our vanity.

If we are depending on others for Impressions that compliment us and make us feel satisfied with ourselves and fulfill our constant desire for approval, then we don't really exist except as a functionary of the praise or blame of others.

Even though Impressions are psychological, since they have to do with our responses to what we experience externally and internally, they have a certain kind of material quality that is finer than the other foods and their finer quality means that they have a more powerful effect. Shock, for instance, of a certain type and intensity can literally kill a human being. What we hear, see, read, think and feel constitute Impressions and this is the real world we live in. It is in this world of incoming Impressions, and how we receive them, and how we react to them that we have to learn to live in the right way. Ultimately, even externally generated Impressions are internal events because they fall on our associations to them. How they are digested determines whether they are used for the dissipation of energy or the growth of Essence.

The Work is meant to be the organ of digestion for Impressions but ordinarily Impressions fall on *associations* laid down in personality and we wind up taking everything in the same habitual way over and over again. Associations are actual pathways in the brain that have been sort of imprinted into it and they create a purely mechanical flow of processing Impressions rather like water flowing downhill following the path of least resistance already present. If you see a clown and clowns scare you, your associations will give you an entirely different experience than perhaps a child may have. If you see a person you know you are not really seeing the person, you are experiencing the impressions you have based on the associations you have about that person, whether good or bad. It is our level of Being that determines where Impressions fall. We can receive no new Impressions unless it changes. If we are negative we experience ourselves or others through identification with those negative feelings and subsequently feed on very bad food from our psychology, which is the highest source of food. In order to take Impressions in a new way we have to change our thinking so that we are not seeing them through the distorted lenses and habitual pathways of associations. If, for example, we could see a person we know without the associations of familiarity, we would get a shock. The same is true for ourselves. If we could see ourselves without our usual associations we would also get a shock.

Now the Work depends on these *'shocks'*, therefore, it is precisely at the place of incoming Impressions that we have to bring in the Work ideas and practices to give us a new way of digesting them. In practice this is called giving yourself the *First Conscious Shock*, and it signifies the psychological location where the real beginning of practical Work lies. We have to give ourselves the First Conscious Shock by applying the Work ideas and practices to ourselves as we experience Impressions. The First Conscious Shock must be given intentionally and so it requires some degree of attention otherwise the impression will fall on the machine of personality and its associations and we will get the habitual response to it. However, if there is something more awake at the time we experience an impression and we bring in the Work ideas we can receive it differently and get a new perspective from it.

For example, when we see that familiar person, we can remember the Work idea that all of us are asleep and function mechanically; we are aware that whatever associations we have of them were formed mechanically in the distortions of our own personality and aren't necessarily true; we don't expect that person to give us a response we want or require of them; we don't go with any negative reactions to them, i.e. we refuse to feel insulted or resentful or, on the contrary, even flattered. Or, if we begin to feel depressed and notice, (because we are working), that we have consented to a train of thought leading to self-pity, since we understand the Work teaching, we can simply get off that train and refuse to go with its thoughts. These are two simplistic examples of what is meant by giving yourself the First Conscious Shock at the point of incoming Impressions.

The highest Impression we can experience is the feeling of Real 'I' that comes from within us, from the state of Self-Remembering at the Third Level of Consciousness.

Being born in the Universe we carry the reflection of the Universe within us - a micro cosmos living within a macro cosmos - and therefore we must in some way correspond to it.

"When impressions begin to fall on us to a deeper level, we begin to live in an entirely new world. If you want to live in a

new world you must go deeper – you must get away from the surface world of yourself and this is certainly in one sense painful but in another sense extraordinarily full of meaning and new satisfaction. You then begin to realize what this means: "I am not this 'I',".... We are born in a Universe to which we can respond and which responds to us if we find out the right request to make. We have eyes that respond to the vibrations of light, ears that respond to the vibrations of air. In short we are constructed to take in impressions."
Maurice Nicoll

GOOD HOUSEHOLDER

This part of the teaching divides people into five categories. They are: Good Householder with Magnetic Center, Good Householder without Magnetic Center, Tramp, Lunatic, and Hasnamous. Briefly speaking, Magnetic Center is that faculty which recognizes B Influences and is, therefore, not wholly satisfied with life's A Influences alone.

So, the first type of person, called Good Householder with Magnetic Center, is a conscientious person who is responsible and well-adjusted in life but does not believe that life aims alone will get them what they wish to attain. They do not fully believe in life as an end in itself but they do their duties anyway.

The next type is Good Householder without Magnetic Center. This person is at a lower level of Being than the first, because without Magnetic Center they do not see the real value of things. Nevertheless, they will deal with their responsibilities reasonably.

Tramps are people who have no feelings of responsibility towards anything. *Mr. Ouspensky said: "Among tramps, you will find many artists and poets, etc. who despise good householder but are really at a much lower level and have no feeling of responsibility toward anything and do not understand what a fool is in themselves.* " Unfortunately, Tramps are often attracted to the Work because they mistakenly think it will enhance their mystique as artists or somehow give them an advantage over others but their valuation of it will never be what it should be since their motives are self-serving. And, consequently they won't be able to actually do the Work and persevere in it.

Lunatics are people who think they can change life and other people by enforcing their theories and making laws because they believe they can *do*. They believe that if everyone would just do what they themselves believe is right, everything would be the way it should be. For example, politicians. They don't often come into the Work because they are sure of themselves and self-satisfied. They, also, don't see the fool in themselves.

The last group is called Hasnamous Man. The word is a term Mr. Gurdjieff coined based on a version of the Turkish language. It refers to a person who is smart enough to see that he can gain power over ordinary people by using tricks, machinations and lies. Mr. Ouspensky said: *"Hasnamous men are people whose well-being depends on the non-well-being of other people."* This description may bring to mind some well-known dictators and that wouldn't be wrong but Hasnamous can be on a big scale or a small scale like a tyrannical parent or employer or false teacher.

The idea of these different kinds of people is important because, *"No one must come into this Work who is not in some degree a good householder. This Work is not for Lunatics or Tramps. People who are no good at life, people who are mad in their theories about how life should be run and imagine that by rules and laws people can be changed, are not good householders and are not suitable for this Work....the quality of such people is not right for the inner discipline of this Work." Maurice Nicoll*

He went on to say that the group they were forming was not a hospital or a charitable institution which is a very important concept to understand for yourself and to keep in mind when you want to introduce someone into this teaching.

One of the most important reasons that Good Householder is the only type of person suitable for the Work is that if you can't do a good job of being responsible for your duties in life, including toward yourself, how can you expect to be able to do even more than that. The Work is extra, it is more than what life requires of you.

PART TWO

***

DYING

DYING

In the Work sense, to die means to eliminate that which you have observed and verified in yourself that keeps you asleep. It's very important that you die to the right things and in the right way and, of course, that you don't take this teaching about death in any literal way. If you are practicing the Work in the following ways you will know quite clearly what you need to die to in yourself. It will be the false personality and all of its attributes. It will be identifications, self-justifying, every kind of negative emotion and every form of falsity in you. The aim of this stage of transformation is to purify the emotional center to make it able to receive influences from Higher Centers or the Kingdom of Heaven.

The death of these different aspects of yourself will happen in different ways but all that is required of you is that you apply the practices of the Work to yourself with sincerity. Sometimes you will have to starve a negative emotion to death by denying it your attention over and over again. Sometimes just seeing it clearly will make it wither and die on the spot. Just the practice of self-observation alone will create a separation between personality and your Real 'I' which grows with repeated observations.

Awakening from your own condition of sleep is not a pleasant or easy experience but all progress hangs in the balance. You will find, early on, that the consciousness and freedom you gain with each step is worth it.

The Work doesn't guarantee any specific results with regard to the *'help'* available at higher levels of consciousness because those are decided individually by higher influences. The Work is to prepare you, to make you pure in heart enough to receive, and silent enough to hear, and conscious enough to see, that is, understand what you receive from Higher Centers. Normally we are only randomly and very rarely in this state for only a moment or two. But in this system of awakening consciousness you can *work* for that state and be in it more frequently and for longer periods of time. If you do you will have touched the Third State of Consciousness which is above you right now. But it isn't a permanent state at first, and you will fall back down into lower states until your continued conscious efforts, with help from above, lift you even higher into the relatively stable condition of Balanced Man #4 before your consciousness can become crystalized, in other words, permanent as it is in Man numbers 5, 6, and 7.

Note that your Work efforts must be ongoing and be prepared for this to last for all of your life or at least until the Neutralizing Force of the Work is permanently established and, therefore, your Third Force is no longer in 'life', it is the Holy Spirit. However, doing the Work becomes a joyous endeavor that enriches your experiences and gives meaning to all things. You will be glad to be given the opportunity to practice and continue to grow, so much so that you will embrace all events
given to you and rejoice in your life and the mercy God has shown you.

Self-Observation is something like a bridge between awakening and death. It is definitely the only path to awakening to yourself, both as you are now and as you will become if you persevere. But it includes the first stages of the death of the false self, as well. So far awakening has been about learning this special teaching and its ideas. Now, beginning with the practice of Self-Observation, it becomes awakening to yourself in a practical way, which begins the separation between your personality and your Real 'I', so it includes a form of dying to yourself correspondingly. This will happen gradually and naturally as you awaken leaving the sleeping state behind you. It won't be a smooth consistent path. There will be days when you are fast asleep, completely oblivious to your aim to practice self-observation. Try to keep the work alive in you by reading and thinking about the ideas even when you forget to practice. Also, practice in retrospect and by writing your observations down. And don't let the Work grow too cold because you can lose the thread of it and never find it again. It becomes a matter of valuation and you will find that the more you practice, the more your valuation will grow.

SELF-OBSERVATION

The practical side of the Work begins with and *depends entirely on the practice of Self-Observation.* Absolutely no change is possible without determined, persistent, objective Self-Observation. *Self-Observation is a conscious act that lets a ray of light into your consciousness.* Remember that consciousness can only grow through conscious efforts, of which few are capable. However, Self-Observation is something you can learn to do and, indeed, must do if you desire self-change. Without clear diligent Self-Observation accumulating over time you can't know what you are really like and therefore you can't know what to die to in yourself, or how to die to it in the right way.

You have read that the "Doctrine of 'I's" is the most important idea to understand in practicing the Work, and this is true because unless you see the many 'I's within your own psychology you won't know which to starve and which to nourish. However, the only way you can *see* your multicity of 'I's is through the practice of Self-Observation. That makes *the practice of Self-Observation the most important exercise for self-change in the Work.*

"The whole of the Work starts from a man beginning to observe himself. Self-Observation is a means of self- change. Serious and continuous self-observation, if done aright, leads to definite inner changes in a man." Maurice Nicoll

It can't be over emphasized that Self-Observation is the fundamental and most significant practice in the Work. Understand that absolutely every other Work practice, and every bit of personal development depends on Self-Observation. It is the operative tool for any growth in consciousness because you can't change something that you are unconscious of. It is through Self-Observation that consciousness develops and the evolution from a stimulus-response organism to a Conscious Man or Woman is made possible.

It is said in the Work that Self-Remembering is the most important practice but there is a paradox here. If you try to practice Self-Remembering before you have practiced Self-Observation, and since you have many selves belonging to your many 'I's, which 'self' will you be remembering? Without Self-Observation you can only be remembering the Personality. The reconciling fact is that Self-Observation is a form, or degree of Self-Remembering as is every other Work practice. None of them are full Self-Remembering but all are efforts to lift yourself into the Third State of Consciousness which *is* Self-Remembering. Self-Remembering is a *state* - which you can also practice being in - while Self-Observation is a *practice* that leads to the *state*.

You are not in the Work if you are not practicing Self-Observation. It takes some time and determination to learn the practice correctly but with every effort you make Self-Observation gains strength and clarity. This is the point where the guidance of a teacher with personal experience in this internal exercise would be extremely helpful. The problem is in finding one since you can't see, or, in the beginning verify, that any particular teacher knows what they are talking about. A "teacher" cannot assist you in this practice unless they have practiced Self-Observation themselves. They cannot lead you through unfamiliar terrain. They don't know where or what the obstacles are or how to get around them, or where the side paths are or what there is to see, or what the destination is. Knowledge of the Work ideas isn't enough since you can receive that basic information from a number of sources. Someone with personal experience is the only guide that can lead you in the right direction. I think the best rule to follow in trying to verify the authenticity of any teacher is to evaluate whether or not you are getting instruction that actually helps you to refine, solidify, and expand your own self-observation and therefore your consciousness. Knowledge isn't enough because knowledge and understanding are two different things. Understanding only comes through applied personal practice and the corresponding growth in Being needed to teach this practice.

The example given to us in the Gospels about self-observation is a familiar one.

"Why beholdest thou the mote that is in thy brother's eye, but considereth not the beam that is in thine own eye?" (Matt. 12:3) "In the Greek the word used for the mote is simply 'see'. That is easy to do. But the word used for the beam in oneself is interesting. It means "to take notice of, to detect, to acquire knowledge of, to take in a fact about, to learn, to observe, to understand." Maurice Nicoll

133

There are several obstacles when you begin to try and practice self-observation. The most intractable one is something you probably can't name because it requires a new way of thinking about yourself.

.... *"we take the thing which we call Oneself—that is, myself, yourself—as one thing. We think we are ourselves.*

"Work on Oneself is thus made quite impossible. How can you work on you, if you and you in each case are one and the same thing? But you and yourself are not the same thing. If you and yourself were the same thing, work on yourself would be impossible... A thing identical with itself cannot see itself, because it is the same as itself, and a thing which is the same as itself cannot possibly have a standpoint apart from itself, from which to observe itself.

"I say all this in order to emphasize how difficult it is for people to begin to work on themselves. If a man takes himself as himself he cannot observe himself. Everything is himself. He says 'I' to everything....At one moment he is irritable and rude, at the next kind and polite. But he says 'I' to it all. And so he cannot see it all. It is all one to him....This massive stumbling block lies across everyone's path and long, very long overcoming of it is the task of Work on Oneself. I have watched people in the work often for many years, who have not yet caught a single flash of the meaning of self-observation—that is, people who still take everything that takes place in them as 'I' and say 'I' to every mood, every thought, every impulse, every feeling, every sensation, every criticism, every feeling of anger, every negative state, every objection, every dislike, every hate, every dejection, every depression, every whim, every excitement, every doubt, every fear. To every train of inner talking they say 'I', to every negative monologue they say 'I', to every suspicion they say 'I', to every hurt feeling they say 'I', to every form of

134

imagination they say 'I', to every movement they make they say 'I'. To everything that takes place within them they say 'I'. They continue to talk as they have always talked and say 'I' to it all. They continue to feel and to think as they have always felt and thought, and they say 'I' to it all. To all their manifestations, to all their mechanicalness, to all their inner life, they say 'I'. And since everything is 'I', what is there to work on?...For who can work on 'I' if everything is 'I'? What can observe 'I' if everything is 'I'? The answer, of course, is that nothing can. A thing cannot observe itself. There must be something different in it for the thing to observe itself. And in our own cases, in the case of everyone, if there is nothing in us different from ourselves, how can we observe ourselves, and work on ourselves? For to work on oneself, it is necessary to begin to observe oneself. But if 'I' and 'myself are one and the same, how can this ever be possible?"
Maurice Nicoll

This is the point where dividing yourself into an observed side and an observing side must become a reality. Understanding how to do this is explained in the next section.

"You have heard it said before that "unless a man divides himself into two he cannot shift from where he is. He has to learn to say in the right way: "This is not me—not 'I' ". Now if he takes his negative emotions as a nasty bit of himself, he will not be able to separate himself from them. Do you see why? He will not be able to separate himself from them because he is taking them as himself and so giving them the validity of 'I'....Whereas the case really is that everything in us, practically speaking, is "It"—that is, a machine going by itself. Instead of saying "I think", we should realize it would be far nearer the truth if we said "It thinks". And instead of saying "I feel" it would be nearer the mark to say "It feels"."
Maurice Nicoll

There are other obstacles that also have to be overcome like laziness, or just remembering to practice, or willful defiance, or ignorance about exactly how or why to observe yourself. But if you begin to be successful and you actually observe something in yourself, a monumental challenge will hit you. It will come in the form of a reaction to what you have seen. Most likely you will be horrified or maybe you'll be embarrassed or ashamed. This response will tell you immediately that you are not practicing self-observation correctly because observation must always be *uncritical*. However, if you can manage to be passive to what you observe you will realize that what you have observed *is not you*. Perhaps you will see your personality behaving in a manner that in no way expresses your inner truth. Maybe you will hear yourself lie and not even know why you lied, or see pretense, or you might see how awkward or obnoxious or inappropriately you have acted, or you might hear yourself repeat the same phrase over and over in a conversation.

There are many things that you will observe in the actions of your personality that you will not like to see and this, of course, can be painful. At the same time seeing them is a degree of liberation from them which leaves you with a lighter inner state because you viscerally feel that *you are not what you observe*. To realize this means, first of all, that the observing part of yourself must be a *passive onlooker*.

There are also common mistakes everyone makes in the beginning. You may mistake 'knowing' or 'thinking' for observing. Knowing that you have negative feelings about something or someone is not quite the same thing as observing that you do. Observing includes what you know – that you have these negative emotions - and a perspective that sees these feelings arise mechanically and is aware that they are subjective because everyone else does not share the same negative emotional reaction, therefore, they are not objectively true except in your own acquired psychology. Knowing is a passive mechanical action, whereas, observing is a conscious, intentional action made from a separate perspective.

Thinking is also a passive mechanical act. You can think about yourself all day, and you usually do, without ever observing yourself at all. You have to get behind this thinking and knowing to a perspective that is not them, but can see them happening. There is a fine line of discernment in these matters that only practicing self-observation will reveal to you.

Self-Observation begins with *dividing your attention*. This exercise is most often given in some variation of the following formula: You are sitting on a bench in the park looking at a tree.

Form a perspective outside of your body and observe yourself looking at the tree. Now back that perspective up to include seeing yourself sitting on the bench looking at a tree. Then from a higher perspective see yourself from a distance, in the park sitting on a bench looking at a tree. Go further and see the park in the surrounding area; in the city, the state, the country, the hemisphere, on the spinning earth, etc. *This is the wrong way to practice dividing your attention.* That's not to say it has no value at all. In regard to 'scale' and 'relativity' it may have, but it is usually a misguided exercise or even an intentional trick exercise given by those who don't know how to divide the attention in the right way for the purposes of Self-Observation.

Under ordinary circumstances your attention is mechanically all going in one direction – out of you – including when you are feeling emotions and thinking about something. You are not *conscious* of what you are thinking or feeling or doing, you are simply thinking and feeling and doing mechanically, even if you have some awareness of what you are thinking or feeling or doing. This is the external level of yourself in the world. If you will notice the *incorrect practice* of divided attention given as an example above, is an expansion of your consciousness *in the external world* and no matter how far you can go with it you will always remain in the sense based, physical, external world. Anyone can do this exercise - look at a tree, see yourself looking at the tree; sit in a chair, feel yourself and/or see yourself sitting in a chair. However, this is the wrong direction and use of your divided attention. It really leads nowhere as far as development of Being is concerned.

Perhaps the first movement of Self-Observation involves observing your physical body in an event in the physical world but the part of your attention that is not engaged in your external experience, in order to observe, must be *turned toward your internal experience* not toward your external position. You have to divide yourself into *an observed side and an observing side* quite intentionally. It is a subtle act but *the 'observing part' of your divided attention must always be directed inward toward your inner world,* toward your 'psychological body' where your thoughts and emotions exist, which is your real life.

Don't let yourself be conned by any sort of "teacher" into thinking that external exercises or practices will lead to any spiritual evolution, no matter what experience you have doing them. These are only part of an arsenal of parlor tricks used by false teachers to make an impression, and they will mislead you.

The whole purpose of dividing your attention is so that you can practice Self-Observation according to the Work teaching. There's no need to visualize yourself looking at an external object or feel your body's sensations for the correct practice of Self-Observation.

But, remember, the whole of the Work and any possible evolution or transformation depends on this practice so learn how to do it correctly from the beginning. This is how the practice of Self-Observation must begin. It leads to a more complete form of observing after perfecting this first level is accomplished. Complete Self-Observation will be described in the following material and it does include some kinds of external observation, too. But the primary aim remains revealing to you what is going on inside of you at any given moment while you are also aware of yourself in the world and the event you are engaged in at the same time.

The first movement of Self-Observation begins when you divide yourself into an *observed side* and an *observing side*. This, of course, is an entirely interior psychological exercise. *The observing side observes your personality, which is the thing you call yourself and includes your actions, words, thoughts, emotions, sensations, moods and every psychological activity.* However, the Work teaches you to start with just noticing that the different centers are acting at different times.

"This is based on the teaching that to make a thing conscious begins to change it. As regards the intellectual center, we observe, notice, become conscious and aware of, the kinds of thoughts going on in that center and where we are identified with them. In the case of the emotional center, we observe the taste of the emotions and whether you are identified or not. In the case of the moving center we observe tension of muscles, strained posture and expressions, frowning, clenching, hurrying, slap – dashing, slamming, all of which waste force and influence other centers." Maurice Nicoll

For example, if you are doing some routine physical activity you can observe that the moving center can function without attention and that the intellectual and the emotional centers can be working at the same time. You can be washing the dishes or walking and also thinking random or even intentional thoughts and/or having random, associative or intentional emotions. However, if you accidentally break a dish or trip and fall you can observe how quickly the mechanics of the personality and the emotional center take over and what negative feelings and thoughts follow.

If you follow an unpleasant train of thought you can observe how it leads you to an unpleasant emotional state. When you are not paying attention any thought can enter your mind, any feeling can enter your heart, from any source, and if you consent to it you will find that it generates corresponding emotions and thoughts and then identification with them.

You might have a sad thought and if you go with it and think it you will find that it leads you to sad emotions. You might feel sad for no reason that you can name but if you consent to feel it you will find that sad thoughts follow. In traditional religious teaching this phenomenon is referred to as *Suggestion, Assent, Captivity*. The thought or feeling that enters you is the *suggestion*; going with it in consenting to think it or feel it, is the *assent*; the identification with it that follows is *captivity*. You are then identified. You are then the 'I' that randomly entered your mind or emotions and that you consented to while you were not paying attention. That is, while you were asleep in second state.

It is important to note here that there is no suggestion of demonic possession being implied. That idea puts the responsibility for your actions outside of you which is the exact opposite of this teaching. There is no external force that can enter you and overwhelm you with its evil power making you an innocent victim of it, unaccountable for your own actions. To believe so is a dangerous mental condition.

That being said, this phenomenon of suggestion, assent, captivity, is something that you can observe happening in your psychology but usually, at first, only in retrospect. It brings up some important points. One, that you can practice Self-Observation in retrospect. It is wise to reflect at the end of the day and observe what was going on while you were asleep in second state. It can be very helpful if you keep a notebook to record your observations. It helps you to remember them more fully and with more accuracy. What did you say; how did you react; what were your motives; what were your actions; what emotional states were you in; did you pretend; did you lie by omission or by commission; were you insincere; did you justify yourself; did you gossip or slander anyone; did you have any moment of self-awareness at all or did you sleep-walk through your day wasting every opportunity to awaken? Your whole life will pass by, in this state of sleep, unless you begin to practice Self-Observation. Then a ray of light will be let into your consciousness and you will begin to have the means for real transformative change of Being which will attract change in your life.

Another important point and a powerful tool that can be used to combat the random associations that infiltrate your mind or heart is to understand that you have the power of *thought selection.*

"We were taught from the beginning of this Work to try to stop our thoughts....We were then told some time later that although we could not stop our thoughts, we could select which thoughts we go with and which we separate from. A man can have any kind of thoughts. Any thoughts can come

into a man. In the Gospels it is pointed out that it is not what comes into a man that defiles him but what comes out of a man. Any sort of thought can enter the mind, but whether you identify with it and act from it—or rather, re-act—is another question. How you think and how you act is what comes out of you. The thought that enters the mind is what goes into a man. What he thinks and does from this thought is what comes out of him." Maurice Nicoll

So, please understand that you cannot stop all your thoughts but you always have some power of selecting your thoughts in your inner world. In the Work there is very little that you actually have the power to do.

You are told to observe yourself which you can learn to do and to make your personality passive which is more like not doing. And you are taught other practices that are more concerned with not doing than with doing, because this system teaches that Man asleep cannot *do. Only a conscious person can do.*

It is your acquired personality that acts or that reacts to life mechanically. You are stuck to the very complex machinery of personality, but your Real 'I' is not that machinery. However, a machine cannot *do* in any real sense. It cannot choose. So, there are very few things you can actually do, but selecting which thoughts and trains of thought you consent to is something real that you have the power to do. You don't have to get on any train of thought that comes along; you don't have to say 'I' to any thought that enters your mind; you don't have to talk to them, you don't even have to acknowledge them. You can let any thought that tries to claim your attention just pass by without speaking to it, or saying 'I' to it. It will come back around to try again but you have the power and the right of refusal. This is a very strong

and significant tool that you can and will need to employ in
your personal work.

*"Now, as regards the example given—the selection of 'I's
in yourself and the rejection of other 'I's—there is an
interesting parable about this. You have heard how often the
Work says: "Do not go with wrong 'I's". The parable about
the selection of 'I's is as follows:*
*"Again, the kingdom of heaven is like unto a net, that was
cast into the sea, and gathered of every kind: which, when it
was filled, they drew up on the beach; and they sat down, and
gathered the good into vessels, but the bad they cast away."
(Matthew 13, 47-48) Think what it means to "put the good
into vessels". Have you a vessel? Have you yet attained
through self-observation any power of inner selection—that
is, of throwing away negative 'I's, and negative thoughts and
emotions, and keeping good ideas and feelings and
experiences and discarding the rest?" Maurice Nicoll*

To return to the particulars of practicing Self-Observation,
it was said that you must divide yourself into two - an
observed side and an observing side. The *observed side* is
you, or rather your personality, although no one can see their
personality acting until they start practicing self-observation.
The *observing side* is a perspective with which you can see
your personality interacting with life in the world as you
normally do and be aware of what is going on in your
psychology at the same time. For instance, you can see
yourself being engaged in a conversation while you are also
aware of your inner state, i.e., are you listening, actually
paying attention or are you planning what you'll say next, are
you feeling resentful, or proud, impatient, or embarrassed or
worried?

You can reflect on it later. The first thing is to be aware, to
see. This is the light of consciousness that the practice of

self-observation lets in which allows you to see what is otherwise in the dark absence of awareness. This ray of light is like shining a flashlight in a dark closed room. You may only get flashes of pieces of objects in the room at first, and you may not like what you see, but light means the beginning of *understanding* which the Work teaches is the greatest force you can create.

The quality of the observing side is all important and you must give yourself patience as you learn with effort and thought and experience how to get it right. *It is vital that self-observation be uncritical, impartial, and dispassionate.* That is why if you have a negative reaction to what you observe you can be sure you aren't practicing it correctly. As soon as you have a negative reaction you are no longer observing, instead, you *are* your reaction. *The observing side must be passive.* It must function this way otherwise you will be caught by your reactions and derailed at every moment. You will lose the delicate thread of observation to the power of negative emotions. Therefore, remember not to judge what you observe but to see it clearly and objectively, as from a distance. Remember, you are observing 'IT' which is the mechanical side in you made up of your acquired personality and its many 'I's.

The observing side is called *Observing 'I'*. At first it is small and weak and unformed but with practice it begins to see more clearly and becomes defined and stronger. Observing 'I' is directed inward toward your thoughts, feelings, states, attitudes, which all belong to the observed side. *Observing 'I' stands interior to and above the observed side.* It is outside of your state and is independent of it. It is seeing your state but not feeling your state. Other 'I's that value the observations and the light of consciousness let in by practicing will gather around Observing 'I' giving valuation and force to the Work. They will attract help from above which you will receive with the assurance that it is a gift, not something you created, but a gift specifically for you from the source of the light.

Self-observation is meant to separate Observing 'I' from what it observes.

"Now the idea of the Work is to make one big Observing 'I' that stands outside the Personality and takes photographs of all the 'I's in the Personality. The more photographs you take, the stronger will the Observing 'I' become and the more chances you will have of coming into a new life freed from the compulsion and habits of the old life." Maurice Nicoll

The Work teaches that behind Observing 'I' stands Real 'I', and behind Real 'I' stands God.

Some of the things self-observation will show you is how your personality likes to assert itself, get attention, or maybe it likes to hide from attention, it wants to have the last word, make the funniest or smartest remark, it interrupts, it presumes, it wants to be regarded with favor, valued, and notice how easily it feels insulted, disheartened, offended, critical, angered, envious, superior, embarrassed, or feels inadequate, justified, judgmental, dissatisfied, and endless other negative emotions. Over time you will have the experience of recognizing the same recurring internal activity and states.

Complaining is one thing that everyone can observe and complaining about the same thing repeatedly can illuminate something within yourself that leads to transformation.

"Now supposing that you find that you have always complained of the same thing in everyone, however different from each other the other people may have been—i.e. you have the same complaint against quite different people—what conclusion can you draw from this observation of yourself?

The only conclusion that you can reach is that there is something in yourself that is working all the time of which you only notice the effects or results.

The fault does not lie in the other people against whom you have these continual complaints but in something in yourself that you have not observed. But once you have realized that this reaction of yours is quite typical, and you have always had complaints in exactly the same way, it will give you a shock. It will startle you. You will see that it is this complaining itself that you have to notice in yourself and not what you imagine causes it. Next time that these complaining 'I's begin to resume their customary activity the shock that you had may just be able to give you the emotional force to observe them before they start using your mouth in your name. You will have the shock of remembering yourself. You will have a moment of being separated from these 'I's—that is, you will no longer identify with them. You will see them as something in yourself to which you have been giving full sanction and full belief all this time and which you have been justifying and so nourishing." Maurice Nicoll

One thing you can learn from these observations is how mechanical the personality is and how it acts according to its formed shape, that was formed without your permission. Remember that personality is acquired and not the real part of you that can grow. Personality can change to some degree on an external level but it is only Essence that can grow. You don't have to make Essence grow, you only have to observe your personality and separate from it.

The resulting release of energy from what you would have otherwise been identified with, will be diverted to the growth of Essence. It is the dividing yourself into an observed side and an observing side that is the beginning of this separation necessary for inner development.

146

Very often in the beginning of observation the tendency is to immediately try to change what you have observed. This doesn't work. The Work teaches you not to try to change what you observe, although its ideas and methods are used to increase the separation between the observing and the observed sides. But observation alone will gradually make a separation within you between your personality and what belongs to your Real 'I', and it will happen in the right way which may not be at all the way you think it should be. If your practice and motives are sincere the Work will work within you to rearrange your psychology to correspond to your Real 'I'. It is said in the Work that "the light will cure you". This light is the light let into your consciousness from above through the practice of self-observation.

So, instead of trying to change what you observe in yourself, draw the feeling of 'I' out of it affectively depriving it of force. Say to it, *"This is not me, not 'I'. This 'I' is in me but it is not me."* That will give strength to inner separation and to Observing 'I'.

Once you have observed a particular 'I' and have verified its existence, then you can apply this practice. If, for example you observe that you always get negative, i.e., impatient, frustrated, angry, or upset whenever you have to *wait* in traffic, *wait* in line, *wait* for a call or anything else, you then have something specific to work on. Then, the next time you have to wait you will have the consciousness and the time to catch your habitual negative reaction and withdraw the feeling of 'I' from the usual negative emotions by saying, "This is not 'I'" to them which will help you to be passive to them. And then you will be free to choose what you give your attention to and how you act. The effect is so liberating and peaceful you will feel as if a heavy weight has been taken off of you, a tangible lightness inside. Actually, you will feel an influx of energy which is the energy released that would have otherwise been spent in negativity. And you will have practical verification of the beauty of doing the Work.

I had a very powerful experience like this when I first began practicing Self-Observation. I was in a busy grocery store waiting in a long line as I impatiently wanted to get home. There were at least a dozen people in front of me and only one line open for checking out. Everyone was expressing some sort of impatience, including me. I observed myself rolling my eyes, exhaling heavily, shaking my head, tapping my foot and peering around the other people to see what the hold up was. I noticed that the young woman at the register didn't seem to know how to do the job very well. Immediately I felt sorry for her and the pressure she must be feeling with so many customers waiting. But the next second I was back to impatiently wondering why all these people in front of me had to be there just then when I was in a hurry. Then the answer became clear to me in a flash, or I should say a *gift* of understanding, that everyone there was there for the same reason I was. It was after working hours and people were on their way home and had stopped to get something for dinner. In order for that to be different all of these people would have to work and even live somewhere else, which would mean that each one would have to have an entirely different life that meant they didn't work where they worked or live where lived. I suddenly experienced on a grand scale that my impatience was insisting that the whole course of their lives would be changed and therefore, the course of the workings of the entire world would be constructed to accommodate my desires. I was shocked at my arrogance and humbled by my understanding, and embarrassed at my eye rolling, head shaking, sighing, foot tapping mechanical behavior. And I was overwhelmed with compassion for the poor cashier who was doing her best in terrible circumstances. Realizing that I had expected the whole universe to work according to my desires was such a shock that it changed something fundamental in me and I felt a sense of peace and lightness settle over me.

"...let us suppose that you have reached that stage of work in which you can clearly observe that you are negative. This is just where you can work on yourself. The point is that you are now observing a definite thing. You have, so to speak, caught it in the very act, and this is due to your discipline in self-observation, without which work on oneself is impossible. For if you do not observe what is going on in you, if you do not let a ray of light into your inner darkness by the practice of self-observing,
you will never have anything real on which to work. Only through the discipline of uncritical self- observation will you catch sight of something definite to work upon." Maurice Nicoll

The more you let in this light the more you can see what you are really like. Each moment of practice gives you another flash of insight until these small glimpses add up to reveal to you a kind of photograph that develops over time. A photograph of this kind is invaluable for personal change. It forms what is called a Work Memory, which is a different level of memory, one you can't forget because your work on yourself has verified it. It not only gives you something specific to work on in the present and future but you will find that it illuminates the past showing you that you have always been like this. You have always been this kind of person who, for example, has to have control, or is impatient, or vain, or critical, or who lies. It may not be pretty but it is insight that can change you. The Work can change the present, the future and even the past.

I'm not suggesting that the practical application of the Work teaching to yourself is an easy or pleasant path.

"We do not like the idea that we are mechanical or asleep, or not properly conscious, or negative, or a cage full of 'I's. We have no pre-formed associations which can take in unfamiliar and offensive ideas of this kind. So, we resist them and we resent them. Only by observing ourselves and all that goes on in us in the light of such ideas can we make new ... associations.

They are made consciously because internal observation of oneself has to be a conscious act. It cannot take place mechanically. Also, the impressions gained from self-observation are not from the outside world through the external senses but from an internal sense, given but not used, a silent witness in myself, a spectator of what goes on in me, into which I must put more and more consciousness, more and more my feeling of I, by withdrawing it (tediously, with trouble), from what it observes. A gradual concentration of consciousness and the feeling of I begins then at this point, which then becomes Observing I in a practical sense, as a practical experience. One has then started on the difficult strange journey to Real I which lies above Observing I."

"The darkness of ignorance and unconsciousness is to be dispelled by the light of consciousness." Such language appeals to romantic, pseudo-spiritual folk. "Light!" they exclaim, looking upwards, "How wonderful!" Unfortunately, this light is very painful in the way it operates. They find the letting of light into themselves not at all pleasant. They have to see what fools they are. It is just that that is an increase of consciousness. But in every case, whoever it is, it is a very tough business to increase the consciousness of oneself and not at all to one's self-liking. Far from it.

An increase of consciousness of oneself is always at the expense of one's imagination of oneself, of one's vanity, at dire expense of Imaginary 'I', at the expense of all the pictures treasured by the False Personality. For this light of consciousness, which illuminates things in us, seeks eventually to bring about the collapse of everything fictitious and unreal so that a new person can develop." Maurice Nicoll

At the same time to feel yourself becoming more authentic and less judgmental and free of old habitual patterns of negativity is a blessing beyond expression. Whatever you bring into the light of consciousness ceases to have power over you so that when you have developed one of these photographs, pieced together over time, you become free of all that is included in it. Eventually you will see what's behind it in the darkness of your unconsciousness. For whatever you are unconscious of is in the darkness and it has power over you. Unconsciousness is darkness and only the light of consciousness let in by the practice of Self-Observation can cure you. The light overcomes the darkness. It reveals a new man, a new woman.

This new person can begin to understand why the work is called Esoteric Christianity. It is the inner meaning of the teaching in the Gospels which is impossible to grasp *"without work on yourself beginning with self-observation that is without criticism, or self- justification or self-pity.... To awaken, a person must see more and more clearly what he or she is like. This is painful, but it gives us courage to die to ourselves and our self-love. If you cannot see by your own observation, step by step, over a long, accumulating time, what you are like, you cannot awaken to what you are like, and so will never desire to die to what you are like. Your consciousness of yourself will not show any increase. And*

unless you begin to awaken to what you are like, the self-love will continue to have full, undisputed power over you. You will think, of course, that you are having power over yourself. You will be grievously, tragically wrong. It will be your pride, your conceit, your vanity, and the annoyance or violence you feel when these are wounded that have power over you. It will be the idea of your own charm and excellence, your self-esteem, self-valuation, self-importance, your polite superiority, and contempt of others, that will direct you. It will be your inner indifference and downright selfishness and meanness, your envy, jealousy and your desire for power, that will control you. All these giants, the offspring of the self-love, have power over you, not you over them. This silly little imaginary 'I', this imaginary thing you call 'I', makes you imagine that you are marching through life in the multitude of your own cleverness and strength, and that is what is so tragic in us all. No, you are being marched along by these tough, merciless giants. All the aspects of the self-love can torment and make us suffer in hundreds and hundreds of ways, all of them useless.
They spoil our lives. Therefore, we must observe, and again observe, our self-love, and bring it into conscious perception and acknowledge it." Maurice Nicoll

Remember that you are observing the acquired side of you which might more appropriately be called "It". "It" is the mechanical, self–running, automatic, stimulus response organism, that has been created in you by the influences of external life on you since your birth. You have had laid down in you without your consent particular associations, particular views, opinions, and ways of taking things that function mechanically. You can observe the mechanical nature of thoughts, of responses, of feelings, of prejudices, of behaviors, reactions, habits, and so on. All of these associations created in you from your earliest childhood make you a certain kind of person. They give a particular shape to your psychological body, but it is only one form of all possible forms of yourself. If you had been orphaned and given to different parents, or if you were brought up in a different culture your psychological body would have a quite different form, yet you would still be yourself. You would just be another version of yourself. Nevertheless, you take this one particular built up version of yourself as yourself although "It" is not your Real 'I' or your Essence. So, Observing 'I' is observing "It". "It" thinks, "It" feels, not you. That is why you can say to what you observe, "This is not 'I'".

"To see what you take as yourself, to see the machine of responses, the machine of behavior, the machine of thoughts, of prejudices, of feelings – this is the idea behind self-observation....But people make the most fantastic and ineffectual attempts to see themselves. They usually think they should smoke or eat less or get up earlier or work harder...Now this Work does not start with anything of that kind. It starts with one's psychological side." Maurice Nicoll

It eventually expands to become full observation and includes the following:

"....you must try to observe everything in yourself at a given moment—the emotional state, thoughts, sensations, intentions, posture, movements, tone of voice, facial expression and so on. All these must be photographed together. This is full observation and from this begin three things: (1) a new memory of oneself, (2) a complete change in the conception one previously had of oneself, (3) the development of inner taste in regard to the quality of what one is observing internally. For instance, by inner taste you can recognize that you are lying or in a negative state

153

without difficulty, although you are justifying yourself and protesting you are not. Here the whole thing turns upon whether you possess inner sincerity or not."

"Self-observation done sincerely from the knowledge of the ideas of this Work lets in light into this inner darkness, this inner chaos of oneself.

That is how self-observation is defined in the Work, for it says that self-observation "lets in light" into oneself....Light is consciousness. This is the beginning of that possible inner transformation of Man that all esoteric teaching, including the Gospels and this Work, is always speaking about through the centuries."Maurice Nicoll

When you can observe your reactions to life as "It" and not as 'I' you are in a position to start organizing and purifying your inner life. As this is accomplished the external side begins to obey the internal side instead of the ordinary condition where the inner side is determined by and obeys the outer side. The outer is meant to correspond to the inner and obey it but can only do so when the inner is developed, and that means purified of negativity. When you act from goodness, that is, from seeing the good of doing so, the internal side develops. This Work is aimed at that kind of self-mastery. One thing must command and one thing must obey and the Work is meant to reverse the life-induced condition of the outer having control over the more authentic, spiritual inner side so that what is most real and pure in you controls the external side. But it is not only external behavior that is meant. Most people can manage to be polite and civilized on the surface when circumstances require it or when appearances are at stake, but this is not enough when you are in the Work.

How you behave internally and invisibly to each other is even more important. This depends on the relative condition of inner purity you possess and this purity is the result of transcending self-emotions, and all of this process begins with and is dependent on self-observation.

"Blessed are the pure in heart for they will see God." *(Matthew 5:8)*

One of the most important factors in self-observation is sincerity. *"To observe yourself you must observe sincerely. Self-observation must necessarily have a certain detachment and this is the beginning of change of being....One can do the same thing from a pure or an impure motive. You can take up something in order to show off or from the love of it. A person can take up this Work, not from any love of it and all it implies and can lead to, but for entirely different reasons."* *Maurice Nicoll*

The word *sincere* literally means *sine-caries* –without decay. Its original meaning is *without rottenness*. So, to observe yourself sincerely means to observe without the rottenness of lying or self-justifying. I will remind you here that self-justifying always lies. You must be sincere in your desire for self-change to even begin to practice self-observation.

Then you must be sincere and scathingly honest with yourself in observing what is going on in your inner life and in your personality in order to see what you are really like, apart from your imagination of yourself. One of the objects of the Work is to break down the imagination you have of yourself – your Imaginary 'I'. Imagination has no real memory so if you only have the unreal memory of Imaginary 'I' you can never see that there is anything wrong with you. In which case you have nothing to work on. But self-observation creates a conscious memory over time called 'Work-memory' which cannot be forgotten because you have verified it with conscious efforts.

155

This brings up the subject of lying. Nothing is worse than to lie in the Work, to the Work, to yourself or others about your work, and especially to your teacher in the Work. All forms of lying kill Essence. Essence is the only part of you that has the possibility of growth in the process of development of Being. Killing it by lying goes against your own aims and efforts making all your work futile.

We all lie, sometimes without even being aware of it. Aside from overt lying there is pretense which is also lying. Pretense is something we all do just from the standpoint alone of having an imaginary 'I' and saying 'I' to every thought and feeling. After all, which 'I' is speaking and is it acquainted with the opposite 'I' that speaks up at another time?

In addition, we pretend to know what we do not know, we pretend to understand what we do not understand, we pretend to be interested when we are not, we pretend to care when we do not, we pretend to be who we are not, and to have what we don't possess, which in the esoteric meaning of the Ten Commandments is referred to as *stealing* – claiming that something belongs to you that does not. This can mean anything from objects to ideas, knowledge, authority, understanding, position, influence, etc.

We also pretend that we are right, especially through self-justifying, which, remember, always lies. Self-justifying exists to put you in the right; to prove to yourself that you have a valid reason for your attitude, but it doesn't really matter whether or not your justification is based on a valid reason because it is the vanity that has to justify your negativity when all negativity is impure and therefore false. So, justifications being based in personality and arising from self-love can only lie. But this whole Work is aimed at intentionally acquiring humility in which there is no pretense, and no need to justify yourself. If humility isn't part of your aim you're on the wrong path.

In the Sermon on the Mount when Jesus says "blessed are the poor in spirit" the word translated as 'poor in spirit' actually means humble. He is referring to those with humility, those who aren't full of the spirit of false personality with all its vanities. However, in the more recent translations of the Bible and from the pulpits around the world this profound truth has been reinterpreted by those who fail to understand why humility is the condition that belongs to those of whom it is said "for theirs is the Kingdom of Heaven". The politically correct theologians of our time are served by the idea that the literal 'poor' have special access to the Kingdom of Heaven. So, "blessed are the *poor*" has become the common understanding of this scripture and a new translation of the Bible has even left out "in spirit" making the real meaning of this scripture inaccessible. It also becomes incomprehensible and untrue because Christ came for everyone – the literal rich or the literal poor – and the Kingdom of Heaven belongs to anyone who is truly humble in spirit - those who have humility. But, this distorted understanding gives an external standpoint from which they can preach about what to 'do' in the world without having to teach anything they don't understand like internal change, like becoming humble, which is always so much more difficult than 'doing good works'. This is not said to discourage good works but it takes an evolved perspective to discern what 'good works' really means for each individual. Each person is called to contribute to life in their own way but every person is called to become humble which is a consciously developed state. This is because only a conscious man can *do* and only a conscious man knows what to do.

157

Everyone else is working for merit – public or private, which is the opposite of humility.

The process of the Work is meant to slowly eliminate the false personality and the self-love, self-interest, pride and vanity that it is made up of. As each verified observation gathers around Observing 'I', a separation grows between personality and Real 'I' which stands behind and above Observing 'I'.

It is this separation that makes room for the Work to dissolve personality and allow Essence to grow. The Work will begin to change you and you will find that many things that used to make you negative in some way no longer bother you so much. Things that made you angry, resentful, bitter, etc., no longer have power over you and you begin to experience a new state of freedom from the compulsions and habits of life as you have been living it. Life changes for you because you are changed yourself even if your external circumstances remain the same.

"The first result is that you cease to blame life and other people and the second result is that you deeply wish to become another person, a new man, or a new woman. And it is as if all the hosts of heaven were waiting in breathless silence to see whether any man or woman will begin to study this unknown thing and so start on the path of the inner evolution of the new meaning that alone explains our existence on this insignificant planet." Maurice Nicoll

NEGATIVE EMOTIONS

The Work teaches that *"you have a right not to be negative."* There is a very important difference here from saying that *you have no right to be negative,* and you should think deeply about exactly what that difference means. You are not born with a negative part of the Emotional Center. All negative emotions are learned from infancy by imitation of the sleeping people around you and life influences. A crying or fussy infant isn't doing so because it's negative. It's hungry or uncomfortable or in pain, or needs to be held. But learned negative emotions become part of the acquired shape of your psychological body and your personality. That being the case, if the Work taught that you have no right to be negative, that you must not be negative, you would not be able to do this Work. It is the sign of a false teaching that insists you take an oath or make a promise about something you cannot do, for example, keeping to a long fast or a vow of silence. So, in saying that you have a right *not to be negative* the Work both acknowledges that you are and will be negative, but also that you have a choice in the matter and that is your natural right.

"A man—an ordinary man—cannot keep a promise under all circumstances, because he is not one person, but many persons. One person, one 'I' in him, may promise or even bind itself by an oath. But other 'I's in him will know nothing about this. To assume that a man can promise is to assume that he is already one, a unity—that is, a man having only one real, permanent 'I' controlling him and so only one will. But a man has many 'I's and as many different wills....If you still imagine you can do, if you still think you can always remember and keep your aim, then you will make no room for the Work in yourself and the Work will not be able to help you. You will not feel your inner helplessness. If you begin to feel your inner helplessness in a right way, you will feel the need of the Work to help you. How can the Work help you? It can help you only if you begin to obey it." Maurice Nicoll

The Emotional Center functions with faster energy than the other centers – 30,000 times faster than the ordinary functioning of the Intellectual Center. It's a higher vibration of energy and so it has more intensity and speed than the other centers and it burns through energy faster. This makes it harder to observe and separate from, but easier to recognize by taste and strength.

Negative emotions, in particular, have a unique power over you. Their force, which comes from the speed of the emotional center combined with the power of identification, seems to be perceived as some form of strength which accounts for the fact that people like them so much. People like to feel strong because they are not strong. Strength is the power of self-mastery over negative emotions, not being controlled by them. You can easily verify how you are drained of energy after an outburst of negativity. Such actions damage you and others, and can be dangerous, but what they never are is a sign of strength. Indulging in them even vicariously, such as watching violent films, is to the psychology, like eating dirt.

In the Intellectual Center you have some degree of choice concerning which thoughts you agree to think because it functions more slowly. You have the time for choosing which thoughts to go with and some time to disembark from a train of thought you mechanically went with. The Moving-Instinctive Center which functions at the most mechanical level can be taught to some extent, as in catching a ball, but it's speed is still far slower than the Emotional Center.

Just try to catch an emotional reaction before you are identified with it, or are able to stop it, or separate from it. This is especially true if it is a negative emotion. There is nothing so difficult to give up as negative emotions regardless of the fact that they make us suffer. Once again, just try to differentiate yourself from your anger, or hurt feelings, or fear. You *are* angry or hurt, or afraid, or any

160

other negative state you may be in. You have no perception other than that you and your state are one. This means you are identified with your state and all possibilities for change have stopped. We are all held captive to identifications by emotions and especially by negative emotions. They are the glue that sticks the feeling of 'I' to the object of identification. Then we cannot see that the way out is above us.

One of the easiest things to observe in yourself is negativity. Negative emotions have a certain quality of force and a discernable inner 'taste'. For instance, it's hard not to notice when you are angry if you are trying to follow the Work and practice self-observation. In any case, the Work definition of negativity is far more extensive than the ordinary understanding of it. It includes anger, rage, irritation, impatience, fear, spite, disparagement, worry, self-pity, annoyance, complaining, meanness, criticizing, dissatisfaction, grumpiness, discontent, judging, bad moods, rejection, being adversarial, being oppositional, competitiveness, selfishness, lying, self-justifying, sneakiness, betrayal, gossip, slander, touchiness, threatening, intimidation, embarrassment, coercion, envy, duplicity, guilt, disappointment, dishonesty, deviousness, malice, brooding, sadness, and sarcasm, among others. It's a good exercise to try to think of other negative emotions to add to this list.

What they have in common is that they are all self-emotions based on self-love and they all have some degree of violence in them from murderous rage to the vague discomfort of mild irritability or self-pity. All negative emotions lead down to violence at their base. It is this quality of violence that you learn to recognize as a psychological 'taste' when you practice self-observation. You will naturally grow to dislike this taste of negativity no matter how much you are attached to your negative emotions or how much you like your negative states. None of them belong to Real 'I' and the stark difference in the quality of taste can motivate you to starve them out of existence by separating from them, by not saying 'I' to them and not feeding them with the force of identification.

"Remember we have 'I's in us that may destroy our lives. So the Work teaches first of all separation from negative 'I's because they are not you – they are the result of imitating other people, what you have read, what you have been taught, and what you have imagined about yourself. All this gives rise to many 'I's in you which are not really you. So the Work says, "This is not I"....you have to create the feeling and power of saying, "This is not I." Maurice Nicoll

Now, normally people love their negative emotions and even define themselves by them. But, as long as you have a secret attachment to your negative emotions they will hold power over you and will ruin your life causing you all kinds of unnecessary suffering. So, try to notice your negative emotions and states. Observe the condition of your Emotional Center and try to work on some of the worst negative emotions in it.

Negativity is something definite that you can work on. If you observe a negative emotion, even in retrospect, notice what it says, what it suggests to you, where it leads your thoughts, what associations it makes. For example, if you have a disappointing experience a negative 'I' may say "Why does this always happen to me?" It might remind you of other disappointments until you find your mind filled with a litany of thoughts about a lifetime of disappointments that lead you, by association, into a state of self-pity and depression. This is an example of following a train of thought that leads you to a bad place in your psychological country.

Our inner psychological world is just like the outer world with both good places and bad places in it. It becomes extremely important that you avoid the bad places in your inner world just like you would avoid going into a filthy or dangerous place in the outer world. Don't touch those states and don't let them touch you. Especially don't let your inner tongue touch them. If you do the words will come pouring out and you will get swept up in the torrent of negativity. Remember that psychologically speaking, *place is state – where* you are in your psychology is *what* you are at that moment. Many trains of thought will lead you into a bad internal place and there your level of being is determined by your state at the time. Our saving grace in the Work is that once you observe a negative train of thought you don't have to get on it. You don't have to assent to it by saying 'I' to it. You can let it pass right by you or you can jump off as soon as you recognize where you're being taken. Sleeping human beings who are not practicing self-observation don't have this marvelous option. They are stuck being lead around by every passing negative emotion and because of this they deserve our pity and compassion.

"....all that this work teaches about what you must notice and perceive internally can be verified by self-observation. And the more you open up this inner world called "oneself" the more will you understand that you live in two worlds, in two realities, in two environments, outer and inner, and that just as you must learn about the outer world (that is observable) how to walk in it, how not to fall off precipices or wander into morasses, how not to associate with evil people, not to eat poison, and so on, by means of this work and its application, you begin to learn how to walk in this inner world, which is opened up by means of self-observation.

"It is the inner world in which we rise and fall, and in which we continually sway to and fro and are tossed about, in which we are infested by swarms of negative thoughts and moods, in which we lose everything and spoil everything and in which we stagger about and fall, without understanding even that there is an inner world in which we are living all the time. This inner world we can only get to know by self-observation." Maurice Nicoll

The Work teaches many things we have to struggle against but negative emotions are the most important because *negative emotions are always wrong work.* They are like dirt in the emotional center and they foul up all the functions of all the centers including the intellectual and moving-instinctive centers. They must be cleaned away so that you can hear from higher centers within you which can't be heard or perceived in a dark, unclean, dysfunctional environment. Purifying the emotional center of negative emotions is vital to the reception of higher influences. All of the Work teaching culminates in this purifying action.

"You must understand first of all that the purifying of the emotional center has to do with these negative emotions. One must not mix the idea of purity of the emotional center with purity as it is understood in a moral sense. People think that impure emotions always refer to sexual thoughts and that pure emotions consist of never having these thoughts....

Mr. Ouspensky says in "Tertium Organum": "There is a division of emotion into pure and impure. We all know this. We all use these words, but understand little of what they mean. Truly, what does "pure" or "impure" mean with reference to feeling? Only an analysis of emotions from the standpoint of knowledge can give the answer to this. Impure emotion gives obscure, not pure knowledge, just as impure glass gives a confused image. Pure emotion gives a clear, pure image of that for the knowledge of which it is intended. There can be a pure sensuality, the sensuality of the Song of Songs, which initiates into the sensation of cosmic life and gives the power to bear the beating pulse of nature. And there can be an impure sensuality mixed with other emotions good or bad from a moral standpoint but equally making muddy the fundamental feeling. There can be pure sympathy, and there can be sympathy mixed with calculation to receive something for one's sympathy. There can be pure love of knowledge, a thirst for knowledge for its own sake, and there can be an inclination to knowledge wherein considerations of utility or profit assume the chief importance." "All negative emotions are impure in the Work-sense." Maurice Nicoll and Ouspensky

In that regard, wrong inner talking is one of the important things to observe. That means inner talking that is impure, that hates, slanders, criticizes, or in any other way psychologically murders another person. Then there is constant complaining, dissatisfaction and self-pity about everything from life in general to a bad hair day. Observe self-justifying and its power. Observe also lying, envy, resentment, pride, vanity, opinions, gossip, attitudes, contradictions and always the fact of your multiplicity, and condition of mechanical sleep. Observe the actions of false personality, identification, imagination, internal considering, making requirements and keeping accounts and all of your negative emotions taken as a whole, and how all of these automatic self-emotions lead back to self-love. As long as your emotions are generated by self-love you cannot change, you cannot love your neighbor as yourself, or even love God reverently. You can count on the Work to show you individually what you need to see in the study of yourself. In all esoteric teaching self-knowledge is the highest knowledge you can attain because it is the real starting point of self-change, and the starting point of self-knowledge is self-observation.

"The first stages of the Work are sometimes called "cleaning the machine." A person who constantly says: "What should I do?" after hearing the practical teaching of the Work over and over again, is like a man who has a garden full of weeds and says eagerly: "What should I plant in it? What should I grow in it? "He must first clean the garden. So the Work lays great emphasis on what not to do —that is, on what must be stopped, what must no longer be indulged in, what is to be prevented, what is no longer to be nourished, what must be cleaned away from the human machine.

"One of the greatest forms of dirt is negative emotions and habitual indulgence in them. The greatest filth in a man is negative emotion. An habitually negative person is a filthy person, in the Work sense. A person who is always thinking unpleasant things about others, saying unpleasant things, disliking everyone, being jealous, always having some grievance, or some form of self-pity, always feeling that he or she is not rightly treated and so on—such a person has a filthy mind in the most real and practical sense, because all these things are forms of negative emotion and all negative emotions are dirt. Now the Work says you have a right not to be negative. As was pointed out, it does not say you have no right to be negative. If you will think of the difference, you will see how great it is....To be able to feel this draws down force to help you. You stand upright, as it were, in yourself, among all the mess of your negativity, and you feel and know that it is not necessary to lie down in that mess." Maurice Nicoll

You have lower levels and higher levels within yourself. If you are in a negative state you are in a lower level of yourself. Better states belong to higher levels already existing in you. They are already there and it is a matter of choice in deciding what state you live in. You have to choose where to live within yourself. Human beings are given more than needed for living an ordinary life. You only use a small part of your brain, for example. You have unused functions that may occasionally be opened up for just a few moments and you have an experience on a higher level where you can see things from a different perspective. Then you fall back down into your ordinary state. However, you can learn how not to walk in the dangerous and unpleasant places in your psychological country. You can train yourself to avoid such places and you will then begin to live a new life in which you stop blaming others and instead you turn around inside and blame yourself for allowing yourself to walk in lower levels, the bad psychological places in yourself.

Negative emotions are almost always about another person as you will notice when you begin to observe them. These are sometimes easier to see than something like self-pity, for example, so, when you observe that you are negative toward another you can begin to do something about it. First of all, remember that the Work teaches that *IF YOU ARE NEGATIVE IT IS ALWAYS YOUR OWN FAULT*. So, instead of looking at the negative emotion toward the other person only, turn around inside and look at the 'I' in yourself which is the real cause of the negativity. If you were suddenly struck with amnesia you would have no associations connected to this other person and consequently no negativity. It is the negative 'I' speaking in you that you are listening to which is the cause of your negative state. If you allow this 'I' to continue to speak and you continue to listen to it your negative state will grow more powerful as it steals your force. This is the object of all negative 'I's – to steal your force and make you miserable and even ruin your life. But remember, the source of the negative 'I' is in you, not in the other person. Whether you like them or don't like them, isn't the point. It is up to you to allow a negative 'I' about them to have life in your mind and in your heart or not. Any person should eventually be able to pass through your psychology without being mauled or murdered even if you don't like them. This is the *psychological meaning* of "Thou shalt not kill". It's not about liking them, it's about not liking the inner taste of negativity and knowing that it cuts you off from the influences coming down from your higher centers. The cure for this situation is to try to see in yourself the same thing that makes you negative toward the other person. But, at first, look at the 'I' in yourself that is negative and observe how it tries to persuade you to be negative with lies and half-truths.

"Try to observe in yourself what angers you in another person so much that you completely identify with that person and cannot stand him or her. This seeing the same thing in yourself cancels out the violence just as plus one and minus one cancel out. This is the true meaning of the Greek word translated "forgive"—as in "forgive one another". There is no trace of "forgiving" in cancelling. Nothing pseudo is meant. It is all cancelled out as by an electric spark passing between two oppositely charged bodies. The more conceited you are the less you can "forgive" by seeing the same thing in yourself so you will be more inclined to violence, for conceit prevents self-observation. You will be your own punishment as we all are." Maurice Nicoll

Understanding this one idea of such great depth can give you the force you need to advance in the Work because we can only advance through the forgiveness of others. If you can find in yourself what you hate in the other the effect is almost magical. Your resentment dissolves away leaving you shocked at first, then humbled, then free.

"Always remember you are here having already understood the necessity of contending only with yourself. Thank everyone who affords you the opportunity." Maurice Nicoll

One of the qualities of negativity is that it is contagious in multiple ways. You can easily verify that if you are negative with someone they will most likely become negative in return. This is one way. Make an experiment when you are with a small group of people and tell them about a negative experience you've had, whether with your family, your spouse, your doctor, boss or car mechanic, or whatever. You will see how quickly most of them will have had their own similar negative experience that they want to share with the group. This is another way that negativity is contagious. Then there is the intentional provocation of negativity by a group or an individual. History is full of examples of this deliberate incitement as are current events.   The thing to remember is that negativity is more contagious than a virus and can do infinitely more harm. In your own body it will disrupt the thinking, feeling and moving-instinctive functions and can literally make you ill. Gurdjieff taught that about 80% of all illness are due to negative emotions. People can make themselves sick all their lives by constant negative states. They eat you up inside as is the case with ulcers and some cancers. Understand that negative emotions left unchecked will not only be contagious they will attract other negative emotions to themselves until almost nothing else is going on inside you and they will cause you harm in many ways including making your physical body sick.

"Psychic energy in the wrong place acts as a poison. When we are negative we poison ourselves and we poison our bodies—and indeed, we poison other people. What can be done when we clearly see a negative Emotion and will not yield weakly to self-justification? I will mention only one thing, among many others, that can be done. Realizing that to permit a negative state to exist unchecked and unarrested is to give it tacit permission to do its worst, and realizing also, as one Eastern system says, that negative emotion, identified with, is similar to a wound in the body, and as serious" ....
Maurice Nicoll

Another characteristic of negative emotions is that they are self- running. They go on and on by themselves if you do nothing to separate from them and they will create new negative emotions long after the original cause is removed. Suspicion is an easy illustration of the way negative emotions twist and distort everything until it is backward, and how they keep on running mechanically adding new material for new negative emotions as they continue.

"Suspicion is an emotional state which soon involves the negative part of the Intellectual Center and the thing we have to understand about the Intellectual Center is that each side of it—the positive side or the negative side—if it works independently of the other can come to any conclusion....then it will bring into operation the negative side, and only the negative side, of the Intellectual Centre, in which case everything will go to prove that your suspicion is right."
Maurice Nicoll

This is because the Intellectual Center uses both the positive and negative halves to evaluate any information in order to form an intelligent conclusion. Using only one half, it can only give a distorted conclusion.

There is nothing easier than to be negative. It is the most mechanical and lowest level of functioning in the negative half of the emotional center. A powerful negative 'I' that you identify with can change you and even damage you permanently. Sometimes negative 'I's exist on the edges of your consciousness just waiting to come forward and speak in your name, and take your force, and make you miserable.

When you are negative you will have a fierce struggle with imagination because imagination will suggest all kinds of things to you that never really happened. It is negative imagination that carries on the negative emotion. That is why your consciousness must be increasingly expanding to include more and more in your awareness. Never underestimate the tremendous power and number of negative emotions.

"They truly are Legion as they defined themselves when Christ asked their name. He said to the evil spirit that was in the man dwelling among the tombs: "Come out of the man, thou unclean spirit." "And He asked him, What is thy name? And he answered, saying, My name is Legion, for we are many." (Mark 8:9) Maurice Nicoll

It takes a great deal of inner strength and consciousness to not be negative - to be passive to your negative emotions - although it may appear otherwise since there is no outward expression of this effort. Most people see their negative state as reasonable and therefore not negative, but this is only a justification. To feel you are right when you are negative is ordinary and serves to empower the negative state. It requires no inner strength or thought. The exceptionally powerful conscious effort it takes to not be identified with your negative reactions, emotions, states and 'I's, is true strength, not the easy surrender to negativity and violence.   The Work teaches that it is not power or sex that rule the world but negative emotions and their violence is the last obstacle that must be overcome in order for a person to evolve. So, it is of the utmost importance that you take negative emotions very seriously and learn to work against them by all the means that this Work teaches.

"You can easily get into the stage in life (and most people remain in this stage) of making for yourselves a pit of negativity, hopelessness, self-pity, internal considering, and also of attributing everything to external circumstances, to outside people – and finally of being totally identified with outside things that have no value at all. Also, one can go down into the pit of making no effort about oneself." Maurice Nicoll

But never forget there is help available to you. Some passages in scripture refer to it:

"God brought me out of the pit, out of the miry clay, and set my feet upon a rock." God speaks through esoteric teaching and *"rock"* symbolizes Truth.

"O God, thou hast brought up my soul from hell, thou hast kept me alive from those who go down into the pit and into the mire." When you feel you have something to hold on to, then you can keep alive.

"Therefore, the quality of the work of transformation.... will depend on the state of the Emotional Centre....The most damaging thing that can happen to it is an attack of violence. Violence acts like an explosion. In extreme cases it may be so intense as to damage permanently. Owing to its repercussions it may affect the reason. Now we are taught that all negative emotions are based on violence and lead down to violence. We know also that violence only breeds violence. Nothing is settled by violence—as witness the world. Many other things have been pointed out, which can all be observed in oneself, concerning violence. One has, of

course, first of all, to become conscious of one's own violence. We have many lesser recurrent attacks of violence. They must be circumvented eventually if we seek to prevent any new life in us from being murdered. All have to work on their violence for all have it though they deny it.... It is due to identifying....Now an attack of violence always disturbs the health. It is a wrong shock in the wrong place. The shock often works out days after in illness or physical trouble."
Maurice Nicoll

In the Work you have two allies when you have to deal with negativity. They are the Intellectual Center and the Moving Center. Take worrying as an example of a negative emotion. Every negative emotion has a corresponding manifestation in the Moving Center and the Intellectual Center. Worry will produce in the Moving Center, conditions where the brows maybe drawn inward, the forehead wrinkled, the mouth pursed or drawn downward. There may be pacing or leg shaking or hand wringing expressing this negative state. Then, in the Intellectual Center there are the thoughts fed by the imagination of every bad outcome possible. Now, you have some control over these two centers that can help you gain some control over the wrong work of the Emotional Center. You can make the body – the Moving/Instinctive Center – relax, first by holding still, and then by putting your attention into each muscle group, starting with the small muscles of the face, and intentionally relax them one by one. This relaxing of all the muscles is a very good exercise for you to practice every day. It helps with tension caused by negative states in general. But in the case of a specific negative emotion it can be an essential factor in getting some control over the state.

Then there are the thoughts which you also have some control over. If you stop the negative imagination and replace the thoughts with some mental activity that requires attention you can have a significant effect on the negative state. In other words, you can use the powers you have over the Moving and Intellectual Centers to affect the wrong work of the Emotional Center's negativity, in whatever form it takes.

"Let me remind you that so much of the Work consists in getting rid of things, of stopping things, of not doing. For instance, if you have some well-developed systems of negative emotion or depression in you, it is useless to say: "Well, what should I do instead?" It is necessary to see and continually separate from the hypnotic power of these well-developed systems of negative emotion. You may be sure that something else will gradually take their place, if you clear away the dirt. You may feel new feelings that you could not have imagined. But the task is that the dirt must be cleared away to expose the new. That is where practical work on oneself lies. It is not a question of "What should I do?" but "What should I not do?" Maurice Nicoll

Another ally in the struggle with negative emotions comes from what the Work calls "buried conscience". One of the objects of the Work is to awaken Buried Conscience which is out of reach underneath our acquired conscience. Acquired conscience is different in different cultures, nations, religions, traditions, individuals and time periods. Buried Conscience is the same in all people and if it could be reached we would know instantly that all negative emotions are wrong. When a person begins to understand that they must work on negative emotions more internally "....*then conscience will help him. But if he works on his negative emotions because he is told he should, or because he is ashamed before others at having them, and so on, then he is working more "externally" upon them, and not genuinely from himself. But for the faint indications of real conscience*

174

that this Work begins to evoke in people, and its inner help,
the struggle with negative emotions would be impossible.
That is, unless we had conscience somewhere in us, negative
emotions would be unconquerable." Maurice Nicoll This is
because only a more powerful emotion can overcome another
emotion. The intellect alone cannot do this regardless of
reason. Only a higher emotion can overcome a lower
emotion, like mercy can overcome judgement.

   "Now, begin to feel a little responsible for your own states
and begin to realize what it means to see that we are all
made self-developing organisms and that our self-
development depends on how we behave psychologically,
emotionally, spiritually, towards life. I can take an event
mechanically or I can take the same event in quite another
way, consciously. Here lies the value of the Work for the
power of the negative part of the emotional center is
terrifically strong. The inclination to be negative is very
difficult to overcome and we are foolish if we think otherwise.
Here lies indeed the devil and hell.

   "Now let us talk once more about why the Work speaks so
much about the purification of the emotional center. The
reason is that when the emotional center is altered or
purified from negative emotions you can begin to get help,
you can begin to receive influences of a new kind which help
you to understand much that you did not understand before.
When the emotional center is made better more or less by
your own work on it, you may be given strength from these
Higher Centers in you which are always awake and always
speaking to you. You may be helped by them. I really mean
helped. If we want to try to awaken we must try to observe
our negative emotions which stand in the way of this
awakening about which all esoteric teaching speaks, whereas
to enjoy negative emotions, nourish them in ourselves by

inner talking, is the very opposite to what one has to do to
make it possible to awaken."
"No one can be rising in the scale of being unless he is
leaving violence more and more behind. Eventually in one's
development violence must go." Maurice Nicoll

IDENTIFYING

In the practice of Self-Observation you will find that there
are places within yourself where it seems you cannot be
passive. These places are where you are identified with
yourself. To be '*identified*' means to be stuck or fixed to
something in your personality from which you cannot
separate. It has to do with emotional energy and where you
place your feeling of 'I'. This is not a conscious placing of
'I', of course. It is a presupposition of what your 'I' is which
makes it more elusive to observe than other personality traits,
and more difficult to separate from. It is your emotions,
especially your negative emotions, that are the glue which
sticks your feeling of 'I' to something you are identified with.

"We are told somewhere in Scripture that unless a man
hates himself he cannot understand the teaching of Christ.
Christ said: "If any man cometh unto me, and hateth
not....his own life also, he cannot be my disciple." In the
Greek, the word translated "one's own life" means "soul" or
"psyche". For example, the phrase "to lay down one's life for
one's friends" should be translated "to go against one's own
soul for the sake of one's friends." We can understand that
going against one's soul is equivalent to going against one's
self-love and that to hate one's life is to hate this oneself that
is formed and controlled by the self-love. We can conceive
the soul at our level as a point of intense self-love through

*which we are made to identify most powerfully." Maurice
Nicoll*

Gurdjieff said that identifying is one of the greatest evils,
one of the most terrible diseases that a person has to struggle
with. Identification must be studied down to its roots in
personality and it must be studied, to begin with, in yourself.
Each person is full of pictures and illusions about themselves
and with each of these you are identified. You take them as
yourself. You believe they are you. You may be embarrassed,
or feel self-righteous and justified, or your feelings are hurt,
you're resentful or vengeful, or you're excited, or afraid and
you may simply be your state. Then you and your state are
the same thing. This is being identified. You are not
observing your state, you are your state. You can't move
from one place to another in your psychology because there
is only that one place where you and your identification are
the same and so you cannot change.

When you are identified with a picture you have of yourself
you cannot see it.

*"Suppose you are fastened to the idea that you are a truthful
person. This means that you are fastened to this picture of
yourself. You picture yourself, to yourself, as being always
truthful. So, wherever you are, you take with you this picture.
You have no existence apart from this picture. You are this
picture. It accompanies you everywhere, no matter even if
you are not telling the truth. This makes no difference to the
picture that you have of yourself and to which you are firmly
glued. If for a moment circumstances make you feel you are
not being quite truthful on some occasion, then at once you
will begin to justify yourself and explain and argue and so on
until you feel again quite comfortable inside, and at peace
with this picture which dominates you. This is being
identified with yourself. It is an example belonging to the*

class of identifying with pictures of oneself. Of course, pictures are legion. But everyone has special pictures of himself or herself with which he or she identifies." Maurice Nicoll

Pictures are made of imagination and vanity and they are innumerable. They belong to false personality and are a great source of instability, falsehood, disharmony, and a cause of negativity. The more pictures that you carry around the more you are identified with yourself and the more easily upset you will be.

So, begin to study identification with the study of identifying in yourself because in order to change your position internally you must be able to observe your state. If you and your state are one and the same then you cannot observe it and so you cannot separate from it and move to a higher state internally. If you presuppose that there is only one thing within you that acts then it will be impossible for one thing to command and another to obey. That is why it is so important to divide yourself into an observed side and an observing side. It is the way out of the prison of the false self and freedom from negativity.

"Identification is so common a quality that for the purposes of observation it is difficult to separate it from everything else. Man is always in a state of identification and for this reason he cannot remember himself. 'Identifying' is one of our most terrible foes. It is necessary to see and to study identifying to its very roots in oneself. Identifying is the chief obstacle to self-remembering. A man who identifies with everything is unable to remember himself. In order to remember oneself it is necessary not to identify. But in order not to identify a man must first of all not be identified with himself. He must remember that there are two in him, one that can only observe at first and another that takes charge of

*him at every moment and speaks in his name and calls itself
'I'. He must try not to identify with this other man who
controls him, and feel that he is different from him and that
there is another in him. But unless this separation is made
and continually made, he remains one man and nothing can
change in him." Maurice Nicoll*

Life comes at you as events, one after another, overlapping
each other. But you don't necessarily see the event, you only
experience your reaction to these ever changing events. Once
you have established an observing side you will have created
a separation between your reactions and the observing 'I',
which will give you the opportunity to see the event you are
in.

*"If you can see what you are caught up by as a particular
sort of event, it is an act of attention to do so, and makes it
possible not to identify with it so much. Now ask yourself:
"What event am I in? and am I totally identified with it?"
This puts you in attention. This prevents you from being so
identified with the event. If you can draw back internally
from whatever event you are identifying with in life, and try
to formulate the event—like this: "This is called being
blamed for something I did not do," "This is called losing
one's temper," "This is called being insulted," "This is called
being overlooked," "This is called losing something," "This is
called being disappointed," "This is called being in a mess,"
"This is called being late," etc. etc.—then you will not
identify so much." Maurice Nicoll*

Try not to go with your habitual reactions to the day's
events. Try to receive them without the filters of associations,
of opinions, of attitudes and respond to them consciously,
with intentionality. This would be non-identifying and every
conscious act of non-identifying saves force and helps
Essence grow. You become conscious that you are identified

and reacting mechanically but you can withdraw force from the identification by observing it as an event, not saying 'I' to it, and by separating from it. If you are identified it means that force is being taken away from you. If you do not identify by making a conscious effort it means that you draw force away from what you are identified with.

"As you know, external life makes us identify everywhere and at every point. You go and shout and scream at football or you are terribly worried about the Korean situation. But it is quite useless. You can learn nothing from being identified. In fact, it stops you from understanding anything." Maurice Nicoll

Science has actually proved this point. Studies have shown that if you get angry you lose some of your ordinary intelligence. Now, being angry is the very definition of being identified and if you lose a portion of your intelligence quotient you have less chance of seeing the right choice or making the right action, because the identification keeps you from understanding.

To avoid confusion a very fine quality of discernment is called for when dealing with identification. It's very important to bring *everything* you observe into the light of consciousness especially identifications. You will feel justified in feeling identified whenever you do this but you must remember that just because you can justify something that doesn't mean that it's right. However, there are some things you may be identified with that are justifiable on one level. If, for instance, you are always very upset by child abuse or war or any form of violence, you will not be able to convince yourself that you shouldn't feel that way because there is some legitimate justification for feeling that violence is bad. The whole Work teaches that violence is bad and must be stopped. But brought into the light of consciousness you

can see that if you get angry about it you will not be able to
see a solution to the problem because the violence in your
identification is something like the violence you are against,
and also because your intelligence is compromised by the
anger you feel. This is where that fine line of discernment
comes in. The Work doesn't ask you to blindly sacrifice your
capacity for making value judgements. It simply teaches that
you can't use discernment unless you are looking at
something in the light of consciousness which will change
your perspective. You may see that there is justification in
feeling that violence is bad but with the understanding that
your own anger about it does not change the situation or
allow for change in yourself. Your anger is not only bad also,
it is wrong work and will distort your ability to relate to the
issue intelligently and effectively and perhaps find a solution.
But if you can study your own identifications without
justifying them you may see new possibilities, whereas
before you could see nothing because you were blinded by
your identification. Remember to stop and observe what
exactly is going on in yourself when you hear yourself self-
justifying. Identification always justifies itself.

There are several words translated as "rich" in the Gospels
and not all of them refer to literal wealth. *"In the Gospels the
"rich man" was one who was very identified. We are told
that the rich man cannot enter into the Kingdom of
Heaven…. the greatest work is to lessen this state of always
being identified and to become "poor in spirit".*

*"In practical directions given in the Sermon on the Mount,
after "poor in spirit" comes the word "meek. This word in
Greek means "not to resent your enemies"– hence the
strange expression: "love your enemies, do good to them that
hate you" becomes more understandable if it means not to
resent what they say or do. Last time we spoke of "poor in*

spirit" chiefly from the standpoint of not identifying. But a resentful man is continually becoming identified through resentment. We were speaking of "poor in spirit" as the contrast to the "rich man" which Mr. Ouspensky defined as the identified man, meaning that the rich man is the kind of man or woman very identified with everything, with their virtues, goodness, merit, charitable actions, talents, cleverness, appearance, position, possessions and so, with their setbacks, negative moods, failures, etc. They are identified with the prevailing pictures of themselves."
Maurice Nicoll

What beautiful clarity to understand that the word translated as "meek" in the Sermon on the Mount actually means to be *without resentment*. It doesn't mean having a mousey, amenable, quiet, retiring personality. As with all true instructions on inner development, to be "meek", that is, without resentment, requires great inner strength and an active consciousness, as does not being identified. Obviously if you are full of resentment you are identified with yourself. Therefore, study identification in yourself when you feel resentful, insulted, overlooked, disrespected, and withdraw the feeling of 'I' from it. You are observing "It" – the machine that feels identified. If you can do this you will save energy that would otherwise flow into one identification after another. That energy will nourish Essence and help you to awaken so that you will no longer only be used by life. When you practice self-observation you bring everything you observe into the light of conscious awareness where it no longer has any power over you. Remember that Gurdjieff said that identifying is the greatest enemy we have to overcome and that it is through always being identified that we are kept asleep.

"What you are not conscious of in yourself will control you because you are identified with it. If you can separate from the False Personality then you will change internally and the whole world and all life will change for you correspondingly. If you become more and more conscious of False Personality then a broader and deeper consciousness will release you from a negative and small minded, egotistical bundle of personal reactions, full of self-fears and hopes, foolish ambitions, daily lying, unnecessary unhappiness, stupid judgments, false pride, imbecile vanity, and all the rest. In short, you will move away from this spurious person you have taken yourself as and served as a slave to and begin to approach the great test for man and woman as regards their inner sincerity and integrity and so purity in this sense – the test that if passed leads to Real 'I', that every man, every woman, was born with, but has forgotten, owing to falling asleep on this planet....The work is about regaining the consciousness that is one's right – it is about awakening from Sleep." Maurice Nicoll

When you experience a moment of not being identified you will find yourself in a quiet central place within yourself where you are aware that all sorts of things going on around you are trying to get your attention and take hold of you to drag you down. But for that brief time they cannot touch you, cannot reach you. In this state you will have another feeling of yourself and the freedom that comes from being separate from the traffic of life, of being yourself in it but distinct from it. In the next moment you'll probably be right back in the middle of the traffic but you won't forget what you have experienced and you will want more of it.

"Life is to be met with non-identifying. When this is possible, life becomes one's teacher; in no other sense can life become a teacher, for life taken as itself is meaningless,

*but taken as an exercise it becomes a teacher. It is not life
that is a teacher, but one's relation through non-identifying
makes it become a teacher. To take life with non-identifying
does not mean empty acting; it means to act from a real
basis, from aim and from understanding the ideas and
meaning of the Work." Maurice Nicoll*

SELF-JUSTIFYING

Self-Justifying is another obstacle you'll have to deal with.
If you observe that you are negative in any way you will
notice how self-justifying will immediately come to your
rescue to argue in your defense and assure you that you are
right and have every good reason to be negative. It will
become someone else's fault that you are negative because
self-justifying means always putting yourself in the right
even if, on some level, you know you are not.

*"To justify oneself means to take the view that you are right
and maintain it. People even justify their negative states and
discard the witness of inner taste. One way is to deny you are
negative." Maurice Nicoll*

Think for a moment, what is in you that can't admit that
you are wrong? I'm not talking about the everyday occasions
when you are right about incidental facts, I'm talking about
not being able to admit that you are wrong about some
negative emotion you have and its presence, or not admitting
that you are wrong in an argument with someone, or wrong
about your opinion or attitude or perspective or your
justifications for them. What is it in you that can't concede
that you are wrong? It is an important question to ask
yourself to help disarm the power of self-justifying.

Self-justifying also means that you are identified and therefore can't be observing impartially. It is a powerful foe and very tough to stop especially in the case of identification. You will always justify what you are identified with because you believe in it and so you are one with it and cannot separate your Real 'I' from it. But you can become aware that if you find yourself justifying then you must be identified which means you are lying to yourself. Like a bell it can remind you to take a closer look and see what is behind it. Regardless of what the facts are, justifying is twisting them for the sole reason of exonerating you of any wrongdoing and giving you the assurance that you are right. It is never the whole picture.

When self-justifying occurs, it can be helpful to remember that one of the main objectives of the Work is to purify the Emotional Center of dishonesty and it is just as important to remember that *self-justifying always lies.* It rearranges the facts, leaves some out, emphasizes some more than others, therefore, it isn't the whole truth so it is a lie. You can begin by simply noticing that you are justifying yourself and then remember what the Work teaches about it. It will not be possible to stop it altogether at first but observing it will give you an idea of how often this action is taking place. And remember, it doesn't matter if you have a valid life reason to feel negative and justified. It is your response that is important and if you consent to go with your negative 'I's then you are agreeing to *be* the problem and you are then held captive to the lowest level of Being within you, and for that time you are out of the Work and asleep in darkness.

On the other hand, if you understand that the purity of your Emotional Center is at stake and you are able to put your self-emotions and your need to feel justified aside, because your valuation of Work aims exceeds your mechanical reaction, you may see something you would not have seen before, you may understand something you would never have understood before, or you may receive a taste of bliss or some other gift from above that you would otherwise never know.

For example, maybe someone is rude to you and you feel insulted and angered because of it. If you can keep self-justifying from taking hold of you and dragging you down into the pit of your own negativity, you might be able to notice that this person who has offended you is actually rude to everyone, or maybe you can remember an occasion when you were rude yourself, intentionally or not. You might wonder why someone would act that way and perhaps see that they are like a wounded animal or maybe they have serious problems that make them oblivious to other's feelings. That gives you the opportunity to have compassion for them because they are suffering. You might see that they are full of negativity and feel merciful toward them knowing how dark that state is and how lost they must be and unhappy as they spread their negativity around creating more negativity in the world and in themselves. And in your understanding of their suffering you might just be able to forgive them instead of resent them. Maybe you would even be able to pray for them instead of condemn them. However, if all you can do is to keep yourself from the negative emotions their insult would normally incite, by refusing to justify them, for the sake of your own inner purity, then you will experience an indescribable freedom and the sweet taste of a higher inner state. This kind of beautiful liberation begins with and depends on self-observation and subsequently practicing not justifying yourself and your identifications. Don't believe what self- justifying is telling you. It is lying.

First it is important to notice how often you justify your negative emotions and to photograph that fact about yourself. Since we like to feel our negative emotions and believe it is our right to have them, verifying how often you justify them will give you an unflattering shock about yourself. But once you have seen your self-justifying you can begin to work on it.

"Self-justifying and buffers prevent us from seeing contradictions in ourselves. To bear the burden of oneself is to be aware of these contradictions almost continually....You cannot get rid of the burden of yourself except by falling asleep. Awakening is painful. It is not only that we have to bear the unpleasant manifestations of others. We have to bear the unpleasant manifestations of ourselves." Maurice Nicoll

INTERNAL CONSIDERING

Internal Considering is a Work term that refers to an internal psychological condition which is continually considering the self, or more specifically the perception of the self by others. It wonders what impression it is making or will make or has made. It worries that it wasn't given enough attention or understanding or that it's various attributes weren't appreciated. It's afraid it wasn't attractive enough, or amusing enough, or intelligent enough. Were the clothes appropriate and fashionable, was the hair just right, were there visible flaws, social gaffs, or any appearance that was unflattering? And, most importantly, was the self-treated with respect, with deference, with the acknowledgement it believes is its due?

The range of *considerations* is boundless running from whether the self-wielded enough power to whether it had bad breath. All of these *internal considerations* spring from self-love and false personality. They are all forms of identifying. They keep you asleep in yourself, obsessively thinking only of yourself, making you constantly insecure and feeling that you haven't been treated right, that is, according to your own evaluation of yourself. This could easily be called being self-absorbed but the Work term has both a broader and a more specific meaning.

Now, Internal Considering is a form of identifying and the Work teaches that you must study identifying down to its roots beginning with yourself. As you can see the field of study is vast just in regard to how much time you waste in internal considering. It has very serious consequences because behind it all is the feeling that you are *owed*. If you feel that you haven't been treated right, valued appropriately, or given enough attention, then you feel that you are owed those considerations and you begin to keep an account book in your mind with a debt column against anyone who hasn't treated you the way you think they should have. They 'owe you' in your mind. You can even keep an account book against life in general if you feel you haven't been fairly treated by your circumstances in life. Therefore, this activity is called in the Work, *keeping accounts*.

This feeling of being owed and owing nothing yourself stops all possibility of inner growth. It's based in part on having manufactured requirements of people and circumstances according to the pictures you have of yourself. You think you're witty but no one laughs at your remarks; you think you should be in charge but everyone else chooses another leader; you think you are unique but others just think you're weird; you think you're attractive but someone else is getting all the attention; you think you're right but no one agrees with you, etc.

The more requirements you have, the more miserable you will be. Nothing will ever go as you want it to, no one will fulfill your expectations. It may not seem serious but internal considering and making accounts means that you're holding a book of debts in your mind that makes you feel you are owed by others. And if you recall, in the Lord's Prayer it is said, *"Forgive us our debts as we forgive others."* So, then, as long as you hold accounts against others who you feel owe you, are in debt to you, and you have not forgiven them, how will you yourself be forgiven? You can only grow in the Work through the forgiveness of others. That makes internal considering in all its forms a deadly blockade to the Work and puts an end to the possibility of growth.

"A man may feel he is not valued enough and this torments him and makes him suspect others and causes him to lose an immense amount of energy and may develop in him a distrustful and hostile attitude.

Closely connected with this is that form of identifying called making accounts. A man begins to feel that people owe him, that he deserves better treatment, more rewards, more recognition, and he writes all this down in a psychological account-book, the pages of which he is continually turning over in his mind....All accounts of this kind, all feelings that you are owed by other people and that you owe nothing yourself, are of very great psychological consequence to the inner development of a man. That is, unless you cancel your debts, nothing in you can grow. It is said in the Lord's Prayer: "Forgive us our debts as we forgive our debtors." Feeling you are owed, feeling debts, stops everything. You hold back yourself and you hold back the other person. This is the inner meaning of Christ's remark that one should make peace with one's enemy. He says:

"Agree with thine adversary quickly, whiles thou art with him in the way; lest haply the adversary deliver thee to the judge, and the judge deliver thee to the officer, and thou be cast into prison. Verily, I say unto thee, thou shalt not come out until thou hast paid the last farthing." (Matt. 5: 25-26)

If you are going to exact psychologically every pound of flesh or every "farthing" from a man who owes you—that is, if you are going to make everyone apologize and make amends and eat the dust, then you will be under the exacting law that Christ warns you to escape from. You will put yourself in prison—that is, under unnecessary laws—and you will not get out until you have paid on your side for all your own faults. But there is a law of mercy—that is, an influence higher than the literal law of an eye for an eye, which is the law of the man of violence. This is an example of "putting yourself under new influences". Maurice Nicoll

As was said, a person can even make accounts against life itself. You may not feel that you have ever had a fair chance, that your parents or family mistreated you, that you made a bad marriage, that you didn't have the opportunity to go to college or have the career you wanted, that you deserve better circumstances, fewer difficulties, more affluence, and all of this is not only written down in an account book, it is sung as a kind of sad song in the background of your psychology. It may be only a silent sad song or you may sing it openly under the right circumstances, especially if you feel there is someone who will listen and sympathize with you. This is a psychologically crippling condition. Because it is a form of self-pity it is a negative emotion. If you think carefully about it you will see that it is full of resentment, and remember that Christ taught "Blessed are the meek" and that the word translated as 'meek' actually means *without resentment.*

190

These sad songs which often exist in the distant background of your consciousness, sometimes even without words, make you an invalid. Self-pity makes you weak inside leading to an over sensitive reaction to life events. So much so, that if it rains on the day you intended to go on a picnic you can feel that the universe is hostile toward you personally. Thinking that life should treat you better, and that people should treat you better, means that you accumulate a lot of internal accounts every day which builds up a sick past that you drag around with you. It infects you like an illness and gives you a weak Being that cannot overcome this condition of pitifulness in order for you to work on yourself.

"To lead a life of internal considering is to consider only yourself and how people treat you. It leaves out how you treat people." Maurice Nicoll

Even though all people have these sad little songs that they sing. It's just a habit that must be brought into the light of consciousness. This form of self-pity is a kind of private relationship you have with yourself that may come forward especially when you are alone but remember you must observe yourself when you are alone as much as you do when you are with people. In fact, when you are alone you may easily be in the worst company you could keep but you are not even thinking of observing yourself at all.

"You must never feel that you can indulge yourself in your worst negative 'I's just because you are alone and that therefore you can behave as you like in yourself. You must cultivate quite a new idea of your responsibility to yourself in this respect." Maurice Nicoll

You don't have to allow your inner tongue to, articulate your sad songs. You don't have to believe them. It doesn't even matter if their facts are accurate, if your relationship to them is negative, that is, pitiful, it is wrong work. The Work calls life on earth a pain factory and it has no meaning of its own except as an opportunity for evolution. Whatever circumstances you are in, they are exactly the right circumstances for you to use for your inner development and personal transcendent growth.

There is a parable in the Gospels that refers to making accounts which reaffirms the connection between the Gospels and the Work.

"Therefore is the kingdom of heaven likened unto a certain king, which would take account of his servants. And when he had begun to reckon, one was brought unto him, which owed him 10,000 talents. But forasmuch as he had not to pay, his lord commanded him to be sold, and his wife, and children, and all that he had, and payment to be made. The servant therefore fell down and worshipped him, saying, Lord, have patience with me and I will pay thee all. Then the lord of that servant was moved with compassion and loosed him, and forgave him the debt. But the same servant went out, and found one of his fellow-servants, which owed him a hundred pence: and he laid hands on him, and took him by the throat, saying, 'Pay me that thou owest.' And his fellow-servant fell down at his feet, and besought him, saying, 'Have patience with me, and I will pay thee all.' And he would not: but went and cast him into prison, till he should pay the debt. So when his fellow-servants saw what was done, they were very sorry, and came and told unto their lord all that was done. Then his lord, after that he had called him, said unto him, 'O thou wicked servant, I forgave thee all that debt, because thou desiredst me: shouldest not thou also have had compassion on thy fellow-servant, even as I had pity on thee?' And his lord was wroth, and delivered him to the tormentors, till he should pay all that was due unto him." (Matthew 18: 23-34)

Always remember the incredible price you pay when you are internally considering and keeping accounts, believing that you are owed and that you owe nothing yourself.

EXTERNAL CONSIDERING

There is a cure for the problem of Internal Considering and it is called *External Considering*. External Considering is the opposite of Internal Considering but it is more than just thinking of the other person instead of yourself, although that is included. It definitely does not mean just being 'nice' to the other person or 'thoughtful' or especially not doing what you think is best. Regardless of intent these actions are little more than your own self-love acting to receive something in return like merit, praise, or appreciation. After all, you may think the other person needs to talk about their troubles when all they want is to be left alone.

Real External Considering begins with putting yourself in the other's position in a profoundly real sense. You have to think of what the other person's life must be like; what issues and difficulties they have to deal with; what their formative experiences must have been; what their sufferings are. But in order to do this you have to first have observed yourself and understood yourself thoroughly. After you have practiced self-observation for a long enough time to have some real self-awareness you can put yourself in another's position in the Work sense.

Included in the action of External Considering is being aware of how the other person perceives you. You have to know yourself well enough to be aware of your own unpleasant manifestations and how you come across to others. Are you loud, pushy, always trying to make light of things, looking only on the bright side, or prophesying the worst-case scenario, do you always think you're right? This also depends on the self-awareness you've gained through self-observation.

In order to Externally Consider another person you must be able to understand what action is required by consciously understanding him or her. You have to know what is best for them from a higher perspective even if what is best is leaving them alone, or potentially upsetting them by saying 'no' to them. Each case is unique and depends on the success of your own self-observation.

INNER STOP

Part of the grace of the Work is that it gives you tools to use against the mechanical wrong work that you begin to see through self-observation like negative emotions, self-justifying, internal considering and identifying. The first step is, of course, self-observation otherwise you would never know what to work on. But the practice of self-observation by itself alone will create a separation between the real 'I' side of you and the personality 'I' side. This separation is a gift and an essential condition of developing higher consciousness. As the separation becomes more defined and Observing 'I' gets stronger you can taste and feel a new version of yourself that is familiar and more comfortable than the old reactionary personality you have been a slave to. However, the Work is a lifelong process always giving new meaning to every internal and external event of your life making it richer and fresher every day. And making it necessary that you continue to make conscious efforts.

One of the first conscious efforts you can make after you have observed some wrong work or a negative 'I' in you is the practice of *Inner Stop*. It means to become absolutely still within yourself.   You are not trying to stop your thoughts. Stopping all thoughts is not possible. Gurdjieff used to give his students an exercise to stop all thoughts in order to allow them to verify that it is not possible. But you can hold yourself inviolate against any particular thought that wishes to grab your attention by being entirely motionless inside. It has nothing to do with stopping the 'I' itself. 'I's will continue to move in and out of your awareness but in your stillness, you have become invisible to them like a rabbit that freezes when it senses a predator. You notice an encroaching negative 'I' or negative state and instead of trying to banish it you become silent and still inside yourself and therefore are invisible to it. You don't talk to it or contend with it in any way, you simply stay still within yourself which will give you the time to proceed to the next movement which is usually the practice of Inner Silence but may be a different Work practice. However, sometimes you will find the simple act of making Inner Stop, will be all that's necessary to free you, even if the same 'I' returns later.

"*In the practice of Inner-Stop, you stand motionless in your mind. Thoughts pass you, speak to you, ask you what you are up to and so on, but you pay no attention to them.... Now you must note that the Inner-Stop exercise is not the same as trying to stop your thoughts. Try to stop your thoughts; and if you are sincere about your experiences....you will admit it cannot be done. But to stand motionless in your mind is another matter....To practice Inner-Stop in the mind is like making oneself motionless in space. You are not noticed....In your mind you are surrounded by different 'I's. Each wants you to believe you are it. Each wants to speak in your name. Suddenly they cannot find where you are." Maurice Nicoll*

Knowing which Work practice to use in any given situation is the definition of the Work term *"sly man"* which is so often given the wrong interpretation. The Work term "sly man" does not carry the meaning of being devious or sneaky. It more accurately means something like cleaver or wise. The sly man, in the Work sense, knows how to avoid the snares of life 'I's by using the right Work practice for the occasion. Sometimes it may be appropriate to simply observe; sometimes inner-stop is the right approach; sometimes you might want to practice external considering; sometimes remembering yourself is the best solution; sometimes putting your directed attention in some activity is the right move. There are many options available and it is the "sly man" or more correctly the "wise man" who knows which practice to employ to stay awake and walk carefully through the various circumstances of life.

"Doing this Work is like fencing or avoiding blows by skillful counter movements. That is one meaning of sly." Maurice Nicoll

Practicing Inner Stop gives you the opportunity to decide the best course of action.

"Now there are some typical events that are extraordinarily difficult to prevent yourself from losing force to, unless after a time that you see that these events are causing you to lose force, and relate to certain wrong things in yourself....I mean, there are some channels in everyone which, if stimulated by some outer event drain force from you right away. These bad associative places in us must be stopped just as you stop a movement. This is to make inner stop in yourself. This phrase Inner Stop is a Work-phrase of great density of meaning. Let us take an example. You have a

*lot of negative associations with a certain person and before
you came into this Work it may never have occurred to you
that it was these negative associations with this person that
caused you to lose force. I mean, the cause was in yourself.
These associations may go very far into your past, so much
so that you cannot alter them. It is exactly in connection with
such vulnerable places in oneself that one must make what is
called inner stop. I advise you not to try to alter these
associations because you cannot. But you can do one thing
and that is to make inner stop about them so that you stop
inside yourself the fire that is going to ignite the train of
associations.*

*We must lose illusions about being able to change things
and dispose of reactions according to our conceit of
ourselves. Only a blind fool thinks he can control himself
under all circumstances. Therefore, the practice of complete
inner stop, which means also the ensuing practice of inner
silence, is very useful. Remember, a single word can make a
person explode with fury. Why? Because there is here a
mechanical channel of associations that leads directly to a
terrible discharge of negative emotions. Doing this Work is
knowing about where you are weak and trying to avoid the
impact of life on these weak places as far as you can."*
Maurice Nicoll

INNER SILENCE

As with Inner Stop, *Inner Silence* is not meant to be
practiced in a general way. It must be about something
specific like a negative 'I' or state that you have observed in
yourself. Then it is like not touching it, especially with your
inner tongue. If you do then the words will flow out in a river
of negativity. Many negative phrases, justifications and

arguments will be formed by your inner talking that may later find their way onto your literal tongue and you will be caught in the powerful current of expressing your negativity. So, do not touch it, do not listen to it, do not argue with it or engage it in any way. The 'I' will be in your mind and you must be aware of it. But keep inner silence against it which is harder even than keeping outer silence. You may be attacked again and again by these same 'I's but you always have this tool to use against them. Remember, also, that you have the right not to be negative and that if you are negative it is always your own fault.

It isn't possible to stop all of your thoughts and it is conceit that believes you can stop your thoughts at will. But you can stop a particular thought by not saying 'I' to it, not acknowledging it, not giving it your attention, your force or your inner voice, to begin with. This is the practice of inner silence. It means being passive to a negative 'I', not trying to reason it away. Being passive only sounds easy. It actually requires the utmost inner strength, clearly defined aim, and active consciousness to be passive when something very strong inside of you wants to shout. That is why this is called the *Work.*

"It is necessary to observe inner talking and from where it is coming. Wrong inner talking is the breeding-ground not only of many future unpleasant states but also of wrong outer talking. You know that there is in the Work what is called the practice of inner silence. The practice and meaning of inner silence is like this: first, it must be about something quite distinct and definite; and second, it is like not touching it. That is, you cannot practice inner silence in any vague general way, save perhaps as an experiment for a time. But you can practice it rigidly in regard to some distinct and definite thing, something you know and see quite clearly.

Someone once asked: "Is practicing inner silence the same as not letting something come into your mind?" The answer is no. It is not the same. What you are practicing inner silence about is already in the mind and you must be aware of it, but you must not touch it with your inner speech, your inner tongue. Your outer literal tongue likes to touch sore places, as when a tooth hurts. So does your inner tongue. But if it does, the sore thing in your mind flows into your inner speech and unwraps itself as inner talking in every direction. You have noticed of course that inner talking always goes on in negative states and that it coins many unpleasant phrases, which suddenly find expression in outer talking, perhaps long after. In the Work we are told that it is necessary to be careful about wrong outer talking at first, and, later on, about wrong inner talking. Actually, wrong outer talking is mostly due to wrong inner talking.

Wrong inner talking, particularly venomous and evil inner talking, and so on, makes a mess within, like excrement. They are all different forms of lying and this is why they have such strength and persistence. Lies are always more powerful than truth because they can hurt. If you observe wrong inner talking you will notice it is only half-truths, or truths connected in the wrong order, or with something added or left out. In other words, it is simply lying to oneself. If you say: "Is this quite true?" it may stop it, but it will find another set of lies. Eventually you must dislike it. If you enjoy it, you will never lessen its power. It is not enough to dislike liking it: you must dislike it." Maurice Nicoll

For example, let's say there is a person that you dislike. Perhaps they have hurt you or even badly mistreated you. You have many 'I's about what a bad person they are and how despicably they have behaved, and you will have to try to keep silent about the inner talking that goes on in your mind. You may notice that you are rehashing what they did to you that hurt you so deeply. And you will have to keep inner silence toward this inner monologue, even if the facts of it are mostly true. If you can manage to do this you will notice how later on you will be having an imaginary conversation with a friend explaining how bad this person is. And you will have to keep inner silence again. Then you will find that in your mind you are explaining it to your therapist, or the other person's family, or your family, or your doctor, or your neighbor, or the other person's boss, or their minister, or yours.

The point is that this inner talking that is full of accusations, complaining, anger, self-pity, slander, self-justifying, defamation, vengeance, and every other sort of negativity will seek opportunities to express itself in endless ways until you can not only rigidly keep silence against it every time it begins, you will have to learn to dislike the foul inner taste of it and also dislike liking the taste of negativity it gives you.

There is no actual relief in unburdening yourself by rehashing negative events. The potential expulsion of energy when you do so may feel like a release of something that had a grip on you, leaving you feeling calmer. This is only true when you are harboring a wrong relationship to your suffering and it feels like you have relieved yourself when all you are actually experiencing is the aftermath of an explosion of adrenaline and negative energy. You have spent your force and as a result you feel weak, which you are interpreting as relief. However, you have not freed yourself because the negative emotions are still inside of you ready to pour out again as soon as the opportunity arises. It is your wrong relationship to them that must be changed by inner separation from them that will give you real relief and freedom.

Negativity, especially anger, can sometimes feel more powerful than being passive because it is a kind of fighting back. Observe this. It isn't true. Forgiveness is far more powerful and it liberates you from the fight and the pain, and releases the other person, as well. But you have to be able to be passive to your reactions before you can truly forgive. And then you can show others mercy by releasing them from your requirements and accepting their unpleasant manifestations as God accepts and forgives yours.

To summarize, inner silence must be about something specific that you have observed in yourself, and then it means not touching it with your inner speech. It isn't always inner talking about another person, it may be fears, or insecurity or many other negative thoughts or feelings but once you have recognized it you can begin to be free of it by keeping silent within yourself about it.

SUFFERING

"People imagine they have something to sacrifice. There is only one thing they have to sacrifice and that is their suffering. A man in this Work must eventually begin to know what Conscious Suffering is compared with Mechanical Suffering." Gurdjieff

"The Work teaches that we all inevitably, have mechanical suffering and that this is the only thing we have to offer as sacrifice. In order to change, one must sacrifice something....This means simply that you cannot change if you wish to continue to be the same person. To change is to become different. The sacrifice the Work seeks is that of your habitual, mechanical suffering. Of course, people will at this point justify themselves and say they have no such suffering, or that what suffering they have is logical and reasonable.

But notice especially where this teaching begins in regard to what you have to give up. Not with your sins in any ordinary sense, but with what the Work regards as a great, even perhaps the greatest sin – namely, being identified with "Mechanical Suffering". Maurice Nicoll

In life there are two kinds of *Mechanical Suffering* – necessary suffering, and unnecessary suffering. Incarnated life on earth brings with it necessary suffering, for instance, the loss of a loved one, among other things. And you can be sure that every person, no matter what their position or circumstances in life, will at some point experience more of this kind of suffering than they can bear. However, most of our suffering is mechanical, habitual and unnecessary. Think what it might mean to sacrifice your mechanical suffering. All unnecessary mechanical suffering comes from the acquired personality and its inability to get what it wants. For instance, vanity can't be satisfied, internal considering can't be turned off, identification can't be separated from. If through the Work practices you could manage to truly get past your habitual mechanical suffering, that would mean giving up everything that hurts you, all of which you can do without. What freedom that would be.

Fundamentally, all negative emotions are unnecessary suffering. They are based on self-love and include things like having your feelings hurt by how you are treated, feeling insulted or offended, worrying about your relative value, your personal attributes, the impression you make, not getting what you want, having what you don't want, self-pity, and so on. All of this kind of unnecessary suffering falls under the heading of Internal Considering which is a form of Identification. But it is easy enough to see that a change in thinking, that is, thinking in a new way, would end this kind of mechanical suffering. If you aren't concerned about how you are perceived or treated you won't suffer because of it; if you don't get angry or irritable because you aren't getting what you want when you want it; if you accept the conditions of your life as your path to consciousness and therefore have no complaints; if you can't be made to feel impatient because you don't expect the movement of the whole universe to accommodate your personal schedule; if your only fear is having a meaningless existence; if you can forgive because you understand that you need forgiveness also and have been given it already, then you would have sacrificed taking offence, anger, irritability, complaining, impatience, fear, and judgement. And you would be free of the burden and pain these mechanical sufferings cause. All of these things, along with all other negative emotions are unnecessary suffering and sacrificing them means working to raise your consciousness and attaining a level of Being that is free from mechanical suffering.

A cautionary note is due here to say that to cause yourself suffering is the exact opposite of sacrificing the mechanical suffering you do have. You can be sure that life will give you all the suffering you can bear and more, both necessary and unnecessary. So, if you think that anything from fasting to flagellation, from standing for hours to prostrations, or any form of martyrdom, in order to show your devotion to your religion is somehow pleasing to God, you need to understand that these things are the exact opposite of what He wants from you. And they lead to no spiritual development. If you gain any measure of control over the body it serves nothing. Not you and not God whose nature is pure goodness and whose purely good will finds the intentional creation of suffering to be offensive. His only interest is in the purity of your heart. God doesn't need martyrs. People need martyrs. God needs living self-transcendent witnesses to his goodness.

In the Work there is another kind of suffering. It is the suffering you feel when you are aware that you are asleep in life and that you are full of wrong work and that you are helpless to stop it. It comes from the realization that although you are in the Work, you haven't been working on yourself. You have forgotten your aim in doing this Work and the importance of it. This is *Conscious Suffering*. It is a deep and real pain, in part because lost opportunity is lost. You can't get it back. It is the pain that cuts like a knife to your very soul. This pain is not necessary suffering because it is not mechanical, it is outside of life and only known to those who have found their way to this path. It is extra, just like this Work is extra and unnecessary to the living of mechanical life in the world. So, it is something you have to accept in the same way you accept the extra efforts that must be made in the Work. Mechanical Suffering leads to nothing but Conscious Suffering leads to inner change.

"....let us take a clear example from Paul. He has written a letter to his group at Corinth cursing them for not working on themselves. He explains that to feel one has not been working – that is that one has been fast asleep in life and its vexations, daily troubles and therefore identified with the events entering from outside via the senses – this is to suffer in another way. He calls this "godly suffering".

"For though I made you sorry with my epistle, I do not regret it, though I did regret; for I see that that epistle made you sorry, though but for a season. Now I rejoice, not that ye were made sorry but that ye were made sorry after a godly sort, that ye might suffer loss by us in nothing. For godly sorrow worketh repentance unto salvation, a repentance which bringeth no regret: but the sorrow of the world worketh death. For behold, this self – same thing, that ye were made sorry after a godly sort, what earnest care it *wrought in you, yea, what clearing of yourselves..." (2Cor. 8-11)*

"What Paul is saying is that to suffer because you have behaved mechanically can lead to something. And so he says that the suffering of the world leads to death – that is, mechanical suffering. From this brief example one can see what Gurdjieff meant in saying that this Work is esoteric Christianity. Esoteric means simply inner – not obvious. People easily read the New Testament without seeing what is meant. The Work, once you begin to understand what it is saying, opens your mind to innumerable things said in the New Testament. Now reflect on this remark: "The sorrow of the world worketh death." Do you see that in these words is the same idea as "mechanical suffering is useless for self-development and puts us to sleep – that is, death? A man, a woman, must sacrifice their mechanical suffering. What then replaces it? What replaces it is suffering because you are suffering. That is, you must replace the luxury of mechanical suffering by suffering because you still love mechanical suffering."

"In one of the Gnostic books – the acts of John – which are not included in the ordinary New Testament, there is a passage in which Jesus says to his disciples:

"If thou hadst known how to suffer, thou wouldest have been able not to suffer. Learn thou to suffer, and thou shalt be able not to suffer." Maurice Nicoll

Now there is also a practical point to understand here regarding your personal work on yourself. Through the practice of self-observation your consciousness of yourself expands so that you can see that what you blame others for is also in you; what you criticize in others is also in you; what you judge and condemn in others is also in you. For example, if you are blaming someone for judging you, aren't your accusations also judging them? This awareness frees you from judging, criticizing, and blaming others for the suffering you imagine they have caused you. In which case that suffering is canceled out not only because you have observed the same thing in yourself but also because you understand that the other person is also asleep in their mechanics. You liberate yourself from your suffering and also others from your judgements and requirements that they behave consciously.

When you have seen your own condition of sleep it becomes hard to remain blind to the fact that everyone else is also asleep and acting mechanically. How then can you hold anything against them knowing what it means to be asleep and seeing your own mechanical functioning as clearly as you see theirs? You would know that they are stuck in the prison of their own sleep and suffering because of it while you have been given this rare opportunity to awaken. Sacrificing your mechanical suffering means dying to the negativity that keeps you identified and asleep.

INNER SEPARATION

From the moment you divide yourself into an observed side and an observing side you begin to make a separation between your personality and your Real 'I' which stands behind and above your Observing 'I'. This separation is essential to your progress in the Work and your evolution. You must be separated from the wrong work of the machine of personality in all of its manifestations and especially from your negative emotions to make room for the Work to grow in you. All change of Being depends on this separation.

You now have tools to use in increasing this separation which are Inner Stop and Inner Silence, Non-Identifying, not

Self-Justifying, External Considering, becoming Passive to Personality and Negativity, and Self-Remembering. A growing dislike for the 'taste' of negativity also helps but possibly the most important effort you can make to facilitate this separation is learning how to become passive to all that the Work teaches you to be passive to - all that springs from self-love – your need to be right, to be in control, to be appreciated, gratified and self-satisfied.

You can assist this process by trying to consciously put your feeling of 'I' more and more in your Observing 'I' side. As your Self-Observation expands and the Work begins to work in you this vital separation between personality and Observing 'I' grows and makes room for the purified new man or new woman you were born to be. It's something like taking a step up in the ladder of Being. A separation must be made between your former level and the new level, between your former self and the new self, since they are discontinuous. The Work gives you tools to make this separation but it is up to you to use them.

SELF-REMEMBERING

"We have to continually remind ourselves in our private thinking what it means to do this Work. We easily forget. It is not that we willingly forget but that we do not have the force to remember. G. said, "A man is not a man unless he remembers himself. But, when he realizes that he does not remember himself he soon finds that he cannot remember to remember himself. His habits of forgetting himself and being asleep in life are too strong." There is not enough force. We cannot concentrate enough to awaken. In the Work we are often like that, going about all day feeling we are asleep and being unable to give ourselves the First Conscious Shock of

Self-Remembering---which requires an effort of concentration, of inner attention and so enough force. Concentration needs force. When force is running into negative states or daydreams or anxious cares, you cannot concentrate. We become distracted while all sorts of mists, fogs, whirlwinds, thunders, lightening, eruptions of steam, torrents of rain take place within our delicate psychic life, all of which we contemplate with satisfaction. It follows that if our force passes into such "natural" phenomena, our psychic country does not produce much in the way of crops."
Maurice Nicoll

The Work puts great emphasis on what is called Self-Remembering. It is a practice in one sense but more accurately it is a state. If you will recall the Third State of Consciousness is above the sleeping level of humanity. It is the State of Self-Awareness, Self-Consciousness and Self-Remembering where personality with its identifications does not exist. The Work teaches that we must try to remember ourselves at least once a day but it is a very obscure practice for a long time. To begin with, because you have many 'selves' belonging to your many 'I's, trying to figure out which self to remember is a challenge. With that as your starting point you ar bound to get nowhere. Think of the practice more like this: try to lift yourself up, above the turmoil of life events and your reactions to them for just a few moments. Imagine that all of the commotion, issues, and concerns are going on below you and you are not touching them, hearing them or even really seeing them.

"You can think of Self-Remembering from one standpoint as a kind of lifting oneself up from the uproar of things in oneself, or of opening a door and going into another room and shutting the door and sitting down quite quietly. It is a very marvelous thing to experience a moment of not being

identified with oneself, with all this uproar, with all this ever-returning and useless turmoil." Maurice Nicoll

It is called Self-Remembering because it is the recollection of our Real 'I', our true essence and origin. It is remembering something we have forgotten, but that is immediately familiar.

"Self-Remembering is not going against the flood-stream of inner and outer things. It is raising oneself – not contending. Contending is another kind of effort. Self-Remembering is a non-identifying with oneself – for an instant – as if one were merely acting and had forgotten. When one remembers oneself one forgets oneself." Maurice Nicoll

This is a conscious effort that you have to make to practice it, but what you are practicing is to be in the state of Self-Remembering. The practice of Self-Remembering is an action to lift yourself into the *State* of Self-Remembering. At the same time Self-Observation and all of the other Work practices are degrees of Self-Remembering. They are not the state itself but are conscious efforts to lift yourself out of the condition of sleep and they lead ultimately to Self-Remembering. In other words, they all lead to the Third State of Consciousness. This is a very important achievement because according to the Work, the influences coming down from above can only be received in the Third State of Consciousness. Light and help are possible at this level but not at the lower levels of consciousness because the lower levels are polluted with the darkness of negative emotions, the noise of personality, and identifications that make it impossible for the sleeping person to receive them or the unclean environment to accommodate them. Those higher vibrations and influences are of a quality that is too fine to be perceived in the dark coarse environment of sleeping humanity. *"And the Light shineth in darkness, and the darkness comprehended it not.* " (John 1:5) It's not that higher influences can't reach anywhere they will, it's that the two lower states of consciousness, which are both states of sleep, cannot comprehend them. That is why awakening from sleep is essential to the development possible for human beings.

"Everything you build up in yourself by work becomes a transforming cause in the future. To live mechanically on the level of cause and effect is one thing that we have to notice to know about. Here nothing can happen save that the past gives rise to a mechanical effect in the future. If there were no Mercy of God it would work out as inevitable. To regard one's life as nothing but causal is not to grasp the idea that everyone can come into new causal influences, by Self Remembering. Otherwise, there would be only "Truth" and no "Mercy". This idea is expressed in religious literature as "forgiveness of sins". Maurice Nicoll

However, full Self-Remembering remains elusive for a long time partly because you cannot remember yourself if you have only sensual thinking which means you aren't open to any other influences than life influences, and the separation between your personality and your Real 'I' isn't defined enough. Although, you should make a practice of Self-Remembering every day for the sake of reaching up to touch the Third State so you can taste its quality. Self-Observation will inform and refine this practice. In fact, it is critical to it.

"Just to try to remember yourself without a lot of previous work on observing different 'I's in you will be purely theoretical.....you have to see that unless you already have the power to observe how you are taking other people or life situations or life events, you cannot remember yourself."
Maurice Nicoll

WILL

"....the object of all real esotericism is to connect Man with the Will of God and to break him from his own self-will. Maurice Nicoll

We all believe we have will and only have to use it to accomplish what we want to do. After all, we will ourselves to get up in the morning and will ourselves to go to work, among other things. This is another illusion. The Work teaches that every 'I' has its own will so as you move seamlessly from one 'I' to another, your will moves with each 'I'. In reality, your will is fragmented, temporary and sometimes contradictory. There are also larger and smaller wills among your multiplicity of wills. Some of them last long enough for you to accomplish your daily tasks, or maybe not, and some of them last long enough to build cathedrals, create great music and beautiful art. Nevertheless, they are all temporary.

Will is located in the Emotional Center which accounts for its changeable and contradictory nature. It takes focused attention of some duration to actually accomplish anything but this is rare among sleeping humanity. Most are subject primarily to the will of the moment and are consequently unreliable. This means that you can't even depend on yourself for simple things like keeping your word or honoring your promises.

Now, this is important to understand because you must will the Work in order to be able to do it, and even when you can, you will sometimes come up against resistance and doubt when your valuation, coming from willing and verifying your work, will be all you have to keep you going in the right direction. To begin with you must will dividing your attention and practicing self-observation. This produces something real to hold on to at such times. But the concept of *Real Will* in the Work sense is both stronger and more delicate than the way will is usually thought of. The following quotes on Will by Maurice Nicoll and Ouspensky are so beautifully explained that I want to include all of them for the benefit of the reader.

Nicoll has asked Ouspensky "Is it possible to describe what Real Will is like? *He said:" "It is like suddenly seeing the solution to a mathematical problem." Usually we associate the concept of Will with a set jaw, a dogged resolve, etc. This is a negative view of Will. The idea that Real Will is something positive is eventually of great value in personal work. Ordinarily we think of Will as something negative because we conceive it only as being exerted against something. We say often that we will resist this or we will not do that. We tend to associate Will with resistance to something, like brakes to stop something. This is a negative idea of Will and it has its place. But you will see that Mr. O. refers to a different idea of Will. It is something that finds right solutions. It unites separate things, it arranges in right order, and so creates something new. It contains the idea of new possibilities. It is not mere denial, mere negation, mere stopping of everything, but the reaching to a new combination, or a new attainment. It has to do with the certainty that a solution is possible, and with a certain kind of active patience towards the at-present unsolved situation, where one does not as yet see the next connection. I say a certain kind of active patience because it has nothing to do with resignation. Often enough we feel confused, especially after a shock. It seems that everything is scattered, in little bits, without relation, particularly when we have been asleep for a long time and working only in imagination. G. once*

*said that "patience is the Mother of Will". There is some
solution. There is some possibility. It has meaning, or rather,
out of every situation it is possible to get meaning. Things
apparently diverse can be brought into some unity of
meaning. It is like asking and waiting.*

   *"So, we can connect the positive idea of Will with the
attaining of new meaning and not merely with negation and
deprivation. When we begin to realize that Will is delight
rather than privation we begin to realize what aim might
mean---as something worth attaining. Will is connected
mainly with the Emotional Center. It is from the development
of this Center that Will begins. Actually it is a new emotion, a
new insight, very quiet and without violence. It is a unity of
things rather than a splitting up, a synthesis rather than
analysis. Real Will is infinitely flexible.*

*All transformation depends on the idea that you can be under
one set or another set of influences. That is one of the central
teachings in the Gospels, in Christ's teaching. There is a
great deal said about the forgiveness of sins of your neighbor
and so on. Why? One has to see that on one level of living
there can be only the level of cause and effect belonging to it.
But the Gospels and this Work teach that---if you do this
Work---there is a totally different line of cause and effect,
and a transforming force enters your existence.*

   *"It has been said from the beginning of this teaching, that
inner sincerity towards it is the only thing that counts, no
matter how you fail, however badly you do. To pretend, to
imagine you can act as if you believe, is, of all the dangerous
things, the worst. The Work says that to pretend is the worst
thing possible to do, the most deadly thing in its ultimate
effects. Pretending is lying. Lying in this sense destroys
Essence. Essence can only grow through truth, through what*

is sincere. If Essence is destroyed everything is destroyed except nervous excitement. You all act and think and judge as if you know already. The more you think you know, the less you know. When you feel you do not know, you feel deprived of Personality. That is why we have to learn what it means not to be negative in the face of a possible new stage of understanding. You will never get to a new level if you are going to feel negative when your present level is attacked and diminished in importance. Will, in the Work sense, comes from a level above the level one is at, and so is above all self-will and self-importance. Realizing this, you begin to see that Real Will means great meaning and great understanding and great flexibility and a great amount of going against what you thought best. This requires that active patience the Work demands. Patience of this sort is called in the Work the Mother of Will.

"People are often fond of "doing things". This they call will. They like arranging things and so on----doing things "on purpose". This may certainly be right on that scale. But it so often happens that they miss what is being done for them, or not see what is lying at hand, before their very eyes. They go along one straight line and think it is manifesting Will. On a small scale it is, but can you see that it is possible to miss so much by sticking to one narrow line of self-will and mistaking it for Real Will? It is, of course, self-will---- having your own way, being efficient, being first, and so on. But Real Will is different. It is, in taste, very gentle." Maurice Nicoll

PART THREE
***
REBIRTH

REBIRTH

"Jesus answered, Verily, verily, I say unto thee, Except a man be born of water and of the Spirit, he cannot enter into the kingdom of God.
" That which is born of the flesh is flesh; and that which is born of the Spirit is spirit." (John 3: 5-6)\

We must remember that water is one of the symbolic words for 'Truth' in scripture and that 'Spirit' is made of a finer quality of materiality than physical matter. That means we must be reborn of Truth and of Spirit - both above our present level of flesh - to enter the Kingdom of God. To be reborn *in* Spirit is a nebulous concept but somewhat graspable to the ordinary mind. To be reborn *'of the Spirit'* is slightly different and less understandable.

Most Christians believe that going through the ritual of being baptized is all that is necessary to be 'born again.' Of course, there are many who take their new religious beliefs seriously and do try to study and follow biblical teaching and some have dramatic changes in their lives because of their commitment or because the Light reached them in their darkness and saved them from the pit they were in. These are the exceptions and to put them in context without diminishing their devotion, it must be said here that Mr. Gurdjieff said that there has only been one true Christian and his name was Jesus Christ. The rest of us are just aspiring Christians. We can understand this if we attempt to do this Work. That effort will show us the hair-splitting difference between being a 'born again Christian' and being born 'of the Spirit'.

Being born of the Spirit means that it is the Spirit that gives birth to the new man or woman. It doesn't mean that the man or woman receives a new Spirit from another person or gives spiritual rebirth to themselves. It isn't theirs to give. Believing that the ritual of baptism and reciting the Nicene Creed bestows a new spiritual body upon the participant is only superstition. In such cases the individual stays the same which is evidence that there is no spiritual rebirth. If there were, the person would be a new man or a new woman dramatically unlike the person they were before the ritual, with noticeably different behavior, different values, different understanding, and a different Level of Being. But these are not things that can be bestowed by one person upon another.

Your understanding doesn't change just because you have been sprinkled or even submerged in water. That's clear enough. Your understanding can only change with a new quality of knowledge that enlightens the mind leaving your old understanding behind. And without a change in your understanding there will be no change in your behavior or your values or your spiritual nature.

It should be easy to see that another person can't give you a new spirit by putting water on you. These rituals are meant to be symbolic of the real experience, not to replace it. That's why 'water' is involved. In sacred scripture water is symbolic for Truth. The ritual is intended to represent the person being submerged in Truth from the Holy Spirit. If this were an actual experience then the understanding would surely change as well as the person themselves. But no one else can do this for you or give it to you. And besides, it is not you that enters the Holy Spirit, it is the Holy Spirit that enters you according to your understanding.

Your understanding is the result of your conscious efforts to combine Esoteric Knowledge with your Being. It belongs to you and can't be taken away from you, the individual. If you are to be submerged in the Holy Spirit's Truth – that is, born of water - it can only be by your own choice and effort

217

to raise your Level of Being. Then, and only then, can you be "born of the Spirit". And, notice, it is the Spirit that gives birth to you. Your rebirth is a gift of the Spirit from above you, predicated on your being reborn of Truth which is something only you can do for yourself. You can receive knowledge and information from many sources but they only become spiritual Truth when you apply them to your Being to create understanding at that higher level of Holy Spirit Truth.

This Work is Truth which, if applied to yourself, will change your understanding. Your understanding is a product of your Level of Being which is changed by your practice of the Work. This means a real change in behavior, perspective, and your essential nature. Everything will be different about a person transformed in this way. Noticeably, authentically different. You can expect to see stability, individuality, peace, patience, tolerance, humility, a distinct absence of negativity, and an appreciation of life under all circumstances. Whatever other gifts or qualities that are given to those who have attained rebirth are only for them to know. We cannot see what is above us in the Scale of Being and so we can only speculate about what it must be like, although the Work will give you some idea of what can and can't be included in it.

This brings us back to that all-important term, *metanoia*, which is both the beginning of transformation and the result of it. It signifies *thinking in a new way* and proceeds all transformation. It transcends repentance and has little to do with feeling sorry. When we do feel conviction – that is, we know we have done something wrong - we are moved to feel contrite - remorseful. If that emotion is strong enough we are moved to repentance - to seek atonement and forgiveness. If repent meant only to feel sorry and ask for forgiveness our psyche may feel relieved but it would remain unchanged and we would most likely repeat the same behavior again. However, if we understand why we behaved as we did, and the real meaning of our life on earth, and if we have some sense of scale about our position in the Universal Scale of Being, and if we know that in spite of these things we are forgiven by the perfect, loving source of all creation, we cannot help but be transformed in our psychological body in such a way that repeating the same offense becomes impossible. We think in a new way and we have transcended the level of Being that could repeat the behavior for which we felt conviction. This is metanoia – transformation to a new level of Being with a corresponding new mind. It goes beyond repentance and even beyond being forgiven. It is the result of *understanding* that we don't deserve forgiveness, we can't earn forgiveness, but our perfect God with perfect mercy gives it to us anyway. Then the gratitude we experience and the humility we feel create a new transcendent mind in us incapable of our former behavior. It's extremely important to understand this concept because *"everything we do affects us forever." Maurice Nicoll*

SUMMARY

As you can see, and verify for yourself, all of the Work practices depend entirely on Self-Observation. Self-observation is not naval gazing as some might suggest. It is self-study and self-study is the necessary beginning if you want to change the kind of person you are. Through self-observation you develop an Observing 'I' that can see what must be changed for you to become the self you were born to be, and in the process get closer to unity with the Holy creator of your being.

Now, ask yourself, what is it in you that observes? You have made its existence possible through your sincere practice of self-observation, but is it you – the thing that is observed? If there were nothing other than the you that is observed then self-observation wouldn't be possible. If there wasn't something within you, other than, and higher than the observed side then this Work would not be possible and individual evolution would be a myth. But from the very first moment of real Self-Observation you have opened the door to a greater possibility for yourself, and you can verify it for yourself.

Then practicing Inner Stop, Inner Silence, Inner Separation, Non-Identification, Self-Remembering, and stopping Self-Justifying, Internal Considering, Keeping Accounts, Mechanical Suffering, and practicing taking Impressions in a new way without associations, and External Considering - these things become something real you can do to create authentic self-change. All of these efforts are different ways of purifying the Emotional Center which increases consciousness, like cleaning a window lets in more light. That is the aim of the Work. That makes it possible for you to hear, see and receive inspiration from what is higher within you and connected to the spiritual dimension above you where the Kingdom of Heaven reaches up to the level of the Divine and out to you. Without emotional purity this isn't possible.

"It is therefore of great importance to notice one's attitude to the Work and those connected with it and also to notice what one is using the Work for. For example, to use the Work to increase the Personality and its ambitions is to have a wrong attitude. That should be clear enough to anyone who has any power of sincerity and does not justify everything. When the Work forms an emotional point in a person....then

that person begins to touch new influences. It is quite easy to know when this has happened. But to keep this point, he must follow and keep to the "truth" of the Work. He must apply it to himself: and if he loses this point, for a time, he must seek for it again....A person feeling himself asleep, feeling he has lost this point in himself, feeling an emptiness and blankness where he had felt something light, must search for what he has lost all through himself. What is he too identified with? What is he internally considering? What is he lying about? What is he expending on pretense? Where is he justifying himself? When did he last remember himself? When has he last made any effort? What has happened to his aim? How many things has he put in front of the Work? When did he last observe himself attentively and go over his mind? When did he last view himself over the past few days? When did he last think clearly about this teaching and search for new meanings? When did he block some important staircase or corridor in his house by leaving a litter of stuff that he should have sorted out and put in place, or slam some door by haste or irritation and forget to go back and open it again? You can all see what a mess of one's house one can make by behaving in sleep for a short time and how easily one can lose something."
Maurice Nicoll

The purification of the Emotional Center depends on the practices of the Work sincerely applied to yourself, which depends entirely on the correct, persevering, conscientious practice of Self-Observation. There is no other way. There is no other path to higher consciousness or self-realization. It all depends on a purified emotional center which depends on awakening from sleep, dying to the false and negative in yourself, which all depend on honest Self-Observation.

You may have all the knowledge in the world. You may have spent your lifetime studying philosophy, religion and even esotericism. You may even be considered an expert on the subject. But knowledge isn't enough. Esoteric teaching must be applied to your Being with the result of actual change in your level of Being otherwise there can be no understanding. Real Understanding comes from a higher level of Being not from any amount of knowledge.

Many people feel a kind of inauthenticity about themselves and yet they cannot find a path that leads to real change no matter what they try. External changes are easy enough, like imitating the dress and mannerisms of a group they join. But real personal evolution to authentic individuality and spiritual rebirth is an inner journey, although it is the same journey for everyone throughout the ages. Just as esoteric teaching is the same teaching throughout the ages. That's why these teachings can be utilized by any person, anywhere, anytime, who is sincerely seeking the real individual meaning of their life on earth. They will all find the same experiences and verify the same truths on the path called the Work and the result will be the indwelling of the Holy Spirit.

Other books by Rebecca Nottingham

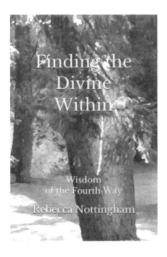

Finding the Divine Within: Wisdom of the Fourth Way

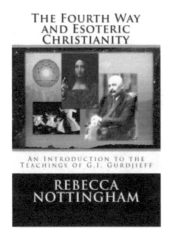

The Fourth Way and Esoteric Christianity

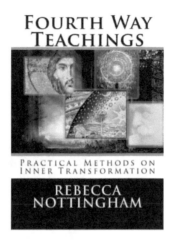

Fourth Way Teachings: The Practice of Inner Transformation

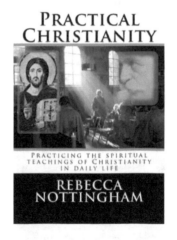

Practical Christianity: Practicing the spiritual teachings of Christianity in daily life

Made in United States
Troutdale, OR
11/15/2023

14603436R00126